Help for Women With Too Much to Do

Pat King

One Liguori Drive
Liguori, Missouri 63057-9999
(314) 464-2500

Imprimi Potest:
Stephen T. Palmer, C.SS.R.
Provincial, St. Louis Province
Redemptorist Fathers

Imprimatur:
Monsignor Maurice F. Byrne
Vice Chancellor, Archdiocese of St. Louis

ISBN 0-89243-294-2
Library of Congress Catalog Card Number: 88-81401

Table of Contents

Introduction

This is a book for the overtired, overburdened, and overextended woman whose energy has been spread too thin by life's situations. For many people this book may appear incomplete because it doesn't tell how to solve all your crises or how to make your loved ones different or even how to be a wonderful Christian.

No, the purpose of this book is far different. It's a book just about you. You know you're tired; it tells you why. You know nothing is as easy as you once thought; it delves into the reasons why this is so.

Some may think the book unspiritual because it doesn't tell you to be brave or to stop thinking about your problems or that you can rise above them. It *says,* unequivocally, that you don't have to wear a cape and be Superlady.

There *are* some solutions to not having enough energy, but they won't change anything or anybody but you. When you've done what the book says, if your husband was difficult when the book began, he'll still be difficult. If your child was impossible, she'll still be that way. If others don't appreciate you or understand you or need you, that won't change, either.

What *will* change will be you. How? Oh, in a lot of ways. Good ways. Interesting ways. Fun ways. Yes, and in spiritual ways, too.

Go ahead, read on. Find out for yourself what there is to be done *just for you*.

ONE

The Day I Ran Out of Energy (and Other Tales)

I was so tired my bones ached. I thought the women would never quit singing. I was the retreat speaker and this was the fifth and final session of the weekend. The women had planned to have a short worship service, then I would speak and the retreat would end.

I've always liked the last talk of a retreat in which the weekend comes together and the retreatants are sent home encouraged in their lives as Christians. But at this retreat the singing went on and on. It was decided that as long as they sounded so good they should rehearse for a program to be presented the following Sunday.

I looked longingly at a table. I was so weary I just wanted to stretch out on it and go to sleep. I was hungry, too. Breakfast had been skimpy and long ago. The night before I'd missed the evening snack after my last talk because a woman had wanted to share her story.

I thought maybe I should join the singing — especially since they were singing one of my favorite hymns, "What a Friend We Have in Jesus." I sang a few words, but it seemed to take too much energy. So instead I rested my head on the back of the chair in front of me and listened to the familiar, comforting words.

Finally they called me to give my closing talk. I had been speaking for about ten minutes when the room began to look peculiar, like an abstract painting. I blinked my eyes and the room came back into focus. Then I began to feel strange. Something was wrong.

"I think I'm going to faint," I told the women. They looked at me as if surely I hadn't said that. "I think I'm going to faint," I said again. Actually what I was experiencing wasn't exactly the same as what you experience when you are going to faint, but it was the closest I could come to describing my feelings. This time a few believed me. Someone got me a glass of orange juice and a piece of cheese, another a chair. I tried to continue on with the talk but it was useless.

I had totally run out of energy.

At home, I described what had happened to my husband, Bill.

"Are you okay now?" he asked.

"I'm fine."

He and the boys were almost ready for dinner when I'd come in. Now the three of them sat down at the kitchen table and I took over. No one said, "You've been through a crisis, why don't you sit down." More significantly, *I* didn't say, "I've been through a crisis, I think I'll lie down." We each had our roles: I served dinner no matter how I felt and they sat at the table expecting the service. (We had so much to learn.)

Two days later I began to feel peculiar again, but this time with something added; there were pains in my chest and I could feel my heart racing. I called the doctor's office. The nurse said it wasn't a heart attack but to keep her posted.

The pains repeated themselves. But the next time the pains came, a strange weakness swept through my body. My heart began pounding. "Katy, come quickly," I requested of my daughter over the phone, "Something's the matter." I called the doctor's office. "Something is wrong."

By the time a nurse was helping me into a bed at the clinic I was so weak I was certain I was dying. *This must be what dying's like,* I told myself as I felt my energy ebbing away. Yet the heart monitor, and later an EKG, showed my heart had no intentions of giving up.

A kind and gentle man, Dr. Lincoln, sat down beside me and introduced himself. "Tell me what's happened," he said, "and then tell me about you."

I told him about the retreat and then tried to think of what he might want to hear about me.

"I have a good, supportive husband and ten children. One of my children, Paul, a twenty-one-year-old, was killed two years ago. I write books, give talks, and I'm a contributing editor to a magazine."

I told him I could remember one other time when I'd felt the same way I'd felt at the retreat. Bill had been in the hospital recovering from open heart surgery. He had been attached to tubes and monitors of every size and shape. As he lay there unconscious he had looked just as Paul had before he died. I'd really prayed that Bill would come through this surgery just fine . . . but I had also prayed for Paul to live.

As I looked at Bill, a terrible realization came over me — that he, too, might die. Those were the first feelings of wooziness I'd ever had in my life, and they had sent me groping for a chair.

That had been ten months ago. Bill's progress compared to his roommate's (not a valid measure, but the only one it seemed I had) was far too slow. Day after day I sat beside his bed feeling terrified. Sometimes I could hardly breathe. There was a funny feeling in my head, as if it were not a part of me.

I held Bill's hand, running my fingers over each vein and knuckle and fingernail I knew so well. I'd loved him since I was fifteen years old. We'd been married for more than thirty-two years. Inside I cried, *Oh God, are you going to take him, too?*

His roommate went home and Bill was still hardly able to talk. The children came to visit and so did our friends, but I felt so horribly alone and afraid. Yet I told everyone I was fine.

When Bill did come home he had a relapse. Medic One, the fire department paramedics, and many neighbors filled our front room. People hovered over Bill; flashing lights from the paramedic truck played against the walls; in the distance the ambulance's siren drew closer. I could feel myself shaking. No one noticed. At last we went off in the ambulance with me in the front beside the driver, and Bill lying so pale and quiet in the back.

By the time we arrived at the hospital, the crisis had passed. Bill was given tranquilizers to take home with him. As soon as the doctor left the room I foolishly opened the bottle and took one. I hadn't had a tranquilizer in twenty-five years, but by this time I was hardly able to cope. The pill knocked me out so quickly I fell asleep leaning against the wall.

After that, Bill's recuperation went so well that two weeks later he was able to walk our daughter, Katy, down the aisle at her beautiful, formal wedding. For myself, all the last-minute preparations and plans of the wedding ran together in a blur of necessities.

Another week later we celebrated Christmas with my parents, our grown children and their spouses, our younger children, and our nine grandchildren — an enormous number of people.

With loving care and lots of rest Bill grew stronger every day. Soon he was driving again and back at work part time. No one, including me, knew *I* needed some rest and probably some tender care as well. In February I did say, ''Bill, let's go to Hawaii for a week or so. I think I need it.'' But we considered the cost and foolishly decided we couldn't afford it.

Instead, Bill, who had lots of energy now that his heart was working correctly, said, ''Let's begin the business we've talked about for so long.'' This meant I had to be busy from morning to night if I was going to care for the family, write, and hold up my end of the new business.

In May I took the eighth-graders on a field trip. We hiked up and down a ravine for most of the day. When it came time to head home I felt too tired to drive. *Don't be silly,* I told myself. But a few minutes on the freeway and I was so tired I could barely hold my eyes open. *Oh God, help me to hang on at least until we get to the rest area*, I prayed. Gratefully, I made it.

''Go amuse yourselves,'' I said to five eighth-grade boys. In two seconds I was asleep. I don't know why it didn't occur to me that this was not normal weariness.

In July I asked Bill to drop me off on the way home from swimming so I could pick some berries. I picked one and found I was too tired to pick another. I couldn't even lift my arm. Somehow I got back to our cabin and fell asleep as soon as my head hit the pillow. *Wasn't that strange?* I thought later.

For more than five years I'd tithed my day in prayer. By August I found that prayer was becoming harder and harder. Not that God seemed far away, just that as soon as I knelt down and began to pray — even first thing in the day — I fell asleep. I gave a talk on prayer to an Episcopalian women's group and felt foolish all the way home. Who was I to talk on prayer when I couldn't even stay awake to pray anymore?

In September Bill and I went to San Francisco, he to a conference, I to be on the television program ''Good Morning, America.'' By now Bill was better than ever. He walked two miles a day and felt wonderful. ''Come on,'' he said the morning after the television program, ''let's go to the early morning Mass at the cathedral across the street and then walk my two miles on those wonderful San Francisco hills.''

''No, I'm too tired.''

''Come on, you'll be glad you did.''

''I just want to sleep.''

''I don't want to go alone. . . . ''

I groaned and made myself go.

We had the same conversation for the next three days and each time I gave in.

One morning halfway through our walk I said, "I'm really hungry. Let's stop for breakfast."

"That's sort of silly," Bill said, "when breakfast is waiting for us at the hotel."

"Yes, I suppose it is."

We kept on walking. It wasn't like us to change our schedule and stop to eat just because one of us was hungry ahead of mealtime.

Looking back, Bill feels terrible that he pressured me and didn't listen to what I was really saying. I don't blame him at all. My body is my responsibility. It was saying sleep, rest, take it easy, eat now. I, too, was the one who really wasn't paying attention. It was two weeks later that I went to that never-to-be-forgotten retreat.

How much of this I told Dr. Lincoln as he sat beside me for over an hour, I'm not sure. I said enough for him to advise me that I was going to have to have a change in lifestyle. What had happened was that I had never recuperated from the strain of Bill's surgery as it related to Paul's death, and I'd just kept on pushing and pushing myself.

Through prayer, mostly my family's and friends' since I was so tired; through close contact with my own doctor; through Bill's new understanding and my own desire to quit being Superlady, the change did come. I've become a different person, not super at all, and I like not being so hard on myself.

For now, that's enough about me. Although I'll tell a few stories about life in our big family, most of this book is really about *you*. About why you're tired and where your energy has gone. When we've looked at your life and your crises we'll talk about the really exciting road back to energy.

I loved the restoration process, and I continue to enjoy the growth involved in understanding myself. I like having enough energy — and so will you!

TWO

Nonreciprocity: What It Means to Be Unappreciated

My friend Dave was left alone to rear five youngsters. One of the methods he used to cope with the logistics of feeding five hungry, growing children (four of them boys) was to shop for groceries every night on his way home from work. He bought food for dinner and the next day's breakfast and lunch. Every evening the food was gone and the children were eagerly awaiting his arrival home with groceries for the coming twenty-four hours.

Time went on and Dave married Kathleen, a lovely, organized woman who had two boys herself. Now there were nine people to feed. That first day back from their honeymoon Kathleen went to the store and bought groceries for a week. When she and Dave came home from work the next night, all the groceries — a whole week's worth — were gone.

Kathleen explained to the children that this had been a week's groceries and next time they needed to make them last. But the children wouldn't listen to her admonishments. No matter how much she bought, they ate it all up the next day. After a number of frustrating weeks Kathleen solved the problem by buying padlocks and installing them on the cupboards.

She also had to develop an innovative system for dealing with laundry. But it required cooperation from kids who "hadn't done it that way before" and who resented her methods. Their participation ranged from refusals to haphazard compliance.

They said she was mean — mean about the food and mean about the laundry, until the everydayness of family life became a battleground. Kathleen confided to me at the end of one weary day that she went to work each morning to rest up. "There," she sighed, "I'm appreciated."

Her words pinpointed the main source of her weariness. It wasn't the shopping or the laundry or even the skirmishes over the food that were so tiring. It was the total lack of appreciation from the very people she wanted so much to help.

That's what nonreciprocity is — being unappreciated. I suspect no one feels it more than the woman who cares for a family — unless it's the woman who cares for a stepfamily.

Nonreciprocity is the root of all burnout, the term people use when they experience severe energy depletion. Not being appreciated makes us tired. It happens when life's situations drain our energy and no one replaces with gratitude the energy that's been taken away.

If you help, listen, support, or sympathize constantly and the people in your life give little or no appreciation, feedback, or even acknowledgment, you will be exhausted. No one can function long without feeling the strain.

Nonreciprocal relationships commonly occur between parents and children, teachers and students, social workers and clients, salespeople and customers, clergy and parishioners, therapists and patients. A fatiguing sense of inequality among peers may also exist between spouses, siblings, relatives, co-workers, or students.

At Home

For many of us it's our families, especially our teenagers, who so often don't appreciate us. We daily give them our lives and they daily fail to understand that we could use some appreciation or some positive feedback in return.

Once I spent my Christmas money on a beautiful (*I* thought) skirt for a daughter who had been complaining she had nothing to wear. "I hate it," she said, "it looks like something *you'd* wear."

A son came home from his first quarter of living and eating at a college dorm. "The food's terrible here at home. At school we have pancakes and sausages every morning and casseroles for lunch and all the chicken I can eat for dinner." (The criticism didn't last long, but it did sting at the time.)

After staying up until the wee hours of the morning making sure that Christmas was going to be as perfect for each child as I could make it, then getting up before dawn to share in the excitement, I looked over to see one daughter sitting in the middle of her Christmas gifts crying loudly. "No one's paying any attention to me." She was right. I put my arm around her and felt sorry for her and sorry for me. There seemed to be no way I could please everyone.

We took two of our children on a lovely trip and one of them quit speaking to us. Anyone who has spent the day in an expensive rented car, the evening in a restaurant where the food costs a fortune, and the night in a luxurious motel with a child who refused to enjoy himself will easily sympathize.

I've not produced enough candy eggs at Easter, shrunk blouses by mistake, typed a term paper wrong, and forgotten to wash gym shorts. Each time I've been made aware of it by tears, complaints, accusations, or hurtful silences.

The years of meals and laundry and tutoring and parties and camping trips and chauffeuring and drum lessons and nursing and praying are all taken as their right. That's the way they've been given. Maybe I should have said, "You are my children. I'm glad to help you in any way I can. But not being appreciated is making me very tired."

On the Job

How many women get up before daylight, fix breakfast for children and get them ready for school or the baby-sitter, walk to a bus or battle an old car, then go to a job where they are not appreciated?

My friend Anne is such a person. At age twenty-five she found herself the total support for herself and her ten-month-old baby. Each day, even before she started on her job as a recreation director in a nursing home, she put in half a day's work just in order to get herself there.

During the long, cold, dark months of winter, when Christmas comes all aglitter to the shopping malls, it came cloaked in gloom for many of Anne's patients. They transferred their despondency to Anne, becoming grumbly, quarrelsome, and fault-finding. The staff that worked for her resented her authority because she was younger than many of them. The staff that worked over her was shorthanded and short-tempered.

One afternoon the craft she had planned for the recreation time didn't work out; the paste had been runny and the handwork messy. One patient after another complained; then someone spilled a pitcher of water. The aides complained to the head nurse and the head nurse scolded Anne in front of the patients. Anne cleaned up in tears. It wasn't her fault. She was doing her best. No one appreciated her. Suddenly she was more tired than she could remember being before. All she wanted to do was to go home and go to bed.

"I can't go to this job anymore," she wailed over the phone. "It's wearing me out. I'm cross with the baby at night and cross with myself." She found that caring for others is a hard job. Not being appreciated makes it exhausting.

In Ministry

Nonreciprocity occurs far too often in ministry. Pastors feel its effects. For laypersons involved in full-time ministry, their spouses probably feel it even more. Missionaries burn out in great number.

In my limited ministry as a speaker, I've felt the nettle of not being appreciated. Once I accepted an invitation to speak at a retreat in a remote part of the country. Just getting there took a lot of energy. It was crowded. Babies fussed. I spent all my free time counseling.

The women, some of whom had traveled a long way to get there, didn't say much. I wanted my talks to touch their hearts, but I couldn't read their faces.

When the retreat was over I went to pack for the long trip home. The retreat coordinator approached me. "The women were certainly disappointed in the retreat," she stated flatly. "Last year's speaker had us marching around the hall and singing until two in the morning and you didn't do anything like that."

I can still remember the way I felt at that moment—like a total failure before God and before each woman. I was embarrassed, humiliated, and suddenly very, very tired.

On the flight home I eventually came to the point in my discouragement where I told the Lord I'd done my best and I trusted him for the outcome of the retreat in the women's lives. I meant it. Even so, the weariness stayed around a long time.

In the end I received mail from almost every woman who was at that retreat. Letters that said how their lives had been changed, letters that erased that terrible time when I felt so unappreciated.

Few Thanked Jesus

Jesus was well aware of the unthankfulness of people. Picture the ten lepers described in Luke 17 who hobbled toward him. They smelled foul, people ostracized them, disease corroded their bandaged limbs. "Jesus, Master! Have pity on us!" they called in loud, distressed voices.

Jesus saw them and was filled with pity. He spoke with compassion, saying, "Go show yourselves to the priests."

His words were enigmatic for these people who were branded outcasts. Yet the lepers were desperate enough to do as they were told. On their way to see the priests, one after another began to feel beneath the bloody bandages a strange tingling in their fingers, toes, hands, and feet, where there had only been stumps moments before. Grabbing at the bulky wrappings, each one pulled them off to find skin — skin as soft as a baby's. "We're healed!" they shouted. Each one's thoughts turned to spouse or children or parents. *I can go home. I can work again. I can live among people!* Their thoughts full of themselves, they hurried away . . . except for one, a Samaritan. Seeing the restoration of his body, he turned back and walked until he found Jesus. He cried out, "Glory to God, I'm healed!" He threw himself at Jesus' feet. Tears ran down his face. "Master, *thank* you."

Jesus looked at the lone man kneeling in front of him. "Ten were cleansed, were they not? Where are the other nine?"

Jesus had done a wonderful thing. The lives of ten people were profoundly changed. Through it he'd wanted God to be glorified. Jesus' words rang with the disappointment that only one had returned to give that glory.

In Luke 8 we see Jesus so weary he fell asleep in a boat in the midst of a storm. He gave and gave and his countrymen plotted his death in return. Jesus knew nonreciprocity.

Friends and Houseguests

One of the most familiar ways that energy gets usurped is through the too-talkative friend. You like her but she comes into your kitchen, sits down, starts talking, even criticizes you or your children, tells you the story she told you last time, rarely asks about you, and if she does she doesn't listen to your answer. When she's gone you feel drained. The reason you feel drained is that you *are* drained. Even the kindest person finds nonreciprocal friendships draining.

Once a woman who was in a desperate situation came to stay for a few days, along with her five children and two large dogs. She rarely lifted a finger. When dinnertime came she took a shower and left me to feed fifteen people by myself.

When she finally found a place to move to I was overjoyed. Yet after she was gone I berated myself for being so glad to see her go. A better Christian wouldn't have felt that way, I told myself.

Now from the perspective of fifteen years I can see that being glad to see her go had nothing to do with my Christianity. Instead, it had everything to do with my personal energy level.

What's going on in your life? What are the situations in which your spouse or children, in-laws, friends, coworkers, the boss, Father, Sister, or the people in your church give you little gratitude or feedback or even acknowledgment? If there is a lot of nonreciprocity in your life, you may be feeling tired and out of energy. You have every reason to feel that way.

Or are you blaming yourself for not being more Christian? Are you saying, ''If only I were a better person I could handle all this''? Either way, keep reading, you're going to like what this book has to say.

THREE

High-ambiguity Situations: When the Available Solutions Don't Solve the Problems

Gertie longed with all her heart to live in Kentucky in her peaceful log cabin, farming the land. Instead, the circumstances of her husband, Clovis, forced her into a crowded Detroit housing project for the duration of World War II. There was no way in the world she could be glad. What was happening to her family tore her apart. There was no way at all for the situation, as she saw it, to resolve itself.

That's what high-ambiguity situations are — situations for which there seem to be no resolutions available. People can burn out or lose energy simply because the choices available do not solve the situation.

High-ambiguity situations may not be enormously stressful in themselves. The stress often comes because of the length of time they go on or the way they oppose what our culture, our faith, or our conscience says is right.

Take the matter of adult children still living at home. It's been said one good way to ruin a party is to wait for a lull in the conversation and then throw out the question, "What are your adult children doing these days?"

In the past a proud father could relate, "Our Jack's gone west. Got a letter from him eight months ago and he's got a fine job setting up for a rodeo. A fine boy, that Jack."

Or a mother might brag, "Mary and her Sam moved clear over to Springfield. They got a fine family started. Three little ones and another one coming at Christmas. That's fifty miles away so we don't see them all that much."

Someone else might add, "Our Roger's joined the Seebees. Oh, the wife misses him, but that boy's seeing the world."

Today the answers to that question may be touched with more reticence than pride. Jack is still at home until he can find himself. Mary and her Sam and the babies have temporarily taken over the upstairs rooms until they can get on their feet. Roger is waiting for his girlfriend to get a job before he moves out.

The parents are uncomfortable with these arrangements. The situation doesn't feel right. It's not the way they'd hoped or planned or supposed it would be. Here they are supporting, cooking for, cleaning up after adult children, when they would really like more freedom and order in their lives now that they're older.

The young adults feel the same ambiguity. Economically stranded, they dislike living at home where the room and board comes with advice, control, lack of privacy, and muted freedom.

Also, there are singles living away from home with strict budgets that allow for little recreation, singles struggling to find friendships within their new world, singles trying to live godly lives in a world without godly principles. The choices before them don't offer pat solutions.

While all the above is not terrible in itself, it's draining on all sides.

Affairs of the Heart

Loving someone who does not return your love is one of the most painful of all situations that do not resolve themselves.

Maureen, a widow, was in her forties when her neighbor's wife became terminally ill. Maureen helped the family, cleaned, prayed, and in time took care of the funeral arrangements. In doing this, Peter, the neighbor, became very special to her.

He relied heavily on her, coming by in the evenings for a snack, some counseling, or cheering up. Maureen was always there, always ready with his favorite foods just in case he stopped in.

Old-timers might have said she "set her cap for him" as she tried every way she could to be helpful. Yet it was more than snaring a man. In the months since his wife's death, Maureen had fallen in love with the man next door. She loved the sound of his voice, the little crookedness of his smile, the seriousness of his grey-blue eyes. She sat in church one Sunday and watched with admiration as he and his children carried the gifts to the altar. He was a wonderful man, and she knew he would eventually ask her to marry him.

When Peter went to a conference, Maureen missed him sorely. After he returned, her friend Andrea called on the phone. Andrea hated to say how she'd heard it, but did Maureen know that Peter was smitten with a woman he'd met at the conference? Her name was Rose. She was pretty and thirteen years younger than Peter.

There was more but Maureen was too numb to remember it. It couldn't be. It just couldn't be. In time she learned that it was true. She felt sick with pain, the way she'd felt when her first husband had died. She loved Peter. She was so sure he had loved her in return.

She couldn't move away; this had been her home for twenty-five years. She continued to look at him, to pray for him, and to miss with her whole heart what might have been.

For over a year her shoulders ached and she felt terribly tired. "I'm just not myself," she told her doctor. The doctor said there was nothing physically wrong with her but asked if there was some stress in her life she'd like to talk about.

She told it all to him, that which she had not been able to tell another person. He listened solemnly, his eyes saying he understood. He didn't give her a prescription to relieve her stress symptoms but he asked her to make another appointment in two weeks to talk some more.

Maureen kept that appointment, and several others. Gradually she began to recover from the ambiguity, the weariness, of unrequited love.

Conflicts in Christian Living

Often Christians find themselves living in ambiguous situations. One part of them wants to do what they are doing. It's so difficult, however, that another part of them would rather not be doing it at all.

My friend Marilyn received a call from her husband, Rudy, who was active with the youth group at church. A woman from their church had just called him and asked if they would take care of her teenage son for two weeks during the summer. Marilyn knew that the woman had quit coming to church and had accused the people in the church of not really caring for her or her son. Now Rudy wanted to show her that they did care. Marilyn also knew that the boy was emotionally disturbed and disruptive. Yet sharing Rudy's desire to heal the breach the woman felt, Marilyn agreed that the boy, Mark, could come.

In two days Marilyn began to realize that she'd made a mistake. Mark had to be watched constantly to keep him from verbally and physically hurting her own three sons. Also, there was the matter of food. Mark wouldn't eat what the family ate, and often Marilyn found she'd been wiped out of a week's supply of ice cream or lunch meat or orange juice.

She decided to go the extra mile, to replenish the groceries with a smile and to rearrange her schedule so her boys wouldn't be alone with Mark. What she did want, though, was some support from Rudy. For some reason he wouldn't give it to her.

"Rudy, Mark drank the two quarts of orange juice I made up last night for this morning's breakfast." Rudy walked out of the kitchen without a word. Later that evening she said, "I really have to watch Mark carefully. He kicked Les pretty hard today." Rudy made no comment. At bedtime she said, "I don't think Mark should have come. It's too hard." Rudy turned away.

Marilyn tried again and Rudy ignored her again. She began to feel extraordinarily resentful, not of Mark but of Rudy. She confided to her prayer partner, "Rudy seems to care more that Mark's mother gets her hurts healed than he cares about his own family. When it comes to people in the church I can't trust him to put us first."

By now Marilyn noticed a strangeness in her body. She felt depleted of energy and her head ached. She could hardly get out of bed in the morning. She had planned to clean the storeroom and she didn't have the get-up-and-go to get started. She needed to run the vacuum but it seemed like too much work.

That's what ambiguous situations do to us. We don't like the way things are going and we don't seem to be able to change them. We begin to feel it in our bodies. All the spirituality in the world won't change the fact that life right now is difficult for Marilyn because of her husband's attitude.

It's easy to forget that in the beginning Marilyn and Rudy shared the same goal — to let Mark's mother know that people do care about her. Inside Marilyn feels hurt, even betrayed. *The trouble is a little thing really,* Marilyn tells herself, so then she feels angry with herself that she can't put up with something so small in comparison to the terrible problems other people face. This kind of feeling only saps more energy.

She could ask Mark's mother to come and get him early, but her conscience won't let her. She could try again to elicit some understanding from her husband, but so far that hasn't worked. The only saving part of the situation is that there is a time limit on it.

Yet for many Christians, the dilemma of not really knowing what the right choice is has no end in sight.

Everyday Life

Ambiguous situations arise all the time, every day. A perfectionist experiences many of them. She wants everything perfect in a world where nothing but God's love is perfect. Her responsibilities at work are increased, her perfect hairdo gets rained on, the car has been in the shop two times and it *still* isn't fixed right, quiet evenings get interrupted by children, guests, or the telephone.

Sometimes Christians who are perfectionists try to pretend they don't mind when their plans don't go perfectly. They smile on the outside when their schedule is ruined, but on the inside the turmoil is so great their bodies grow tense and weary.

Not wanting to go to work and yet needing the money is stressful. Not wanting to face the boss but needing to support yourself is stressful. Not wanting to leave the children in day-care centers or by themselves and knowing you must is stressful. More and more we read in women's magazines of women who quit their jobs to stay home. Yet for every woman who quits, or for every woman who loves her job, there are untold numbers of women who must keep working. No matter how much they want it to be different, a living has to be earned.

For working mothers, telephone calls from home add to the stress. "Mom, Bobby squirted me with the hose and he got water all over the house." "Mom, I'm at some lady's house. I fell off the roof. Here, she wants to talk to you." Or, the most bittersweet of all, "Hello, Mommy, I just called because I miss you."

If you're a parent, trying to find the right sitter adds to the stress. A sitter can greet you at the end of a hard day with, "I can't baby-sit anymore starting tomorrow." They say, "I've been watching little Susie — I don't think you give her enough attention." Or they complain, "I can't control these kids."

Work at home multiplies. No one cleans during the day. Dinner is never ready. Laundry goes unsorted for weeks.

Working mothers often think, *If only I could quit, stay home, and not go through this*. They grow weary from their jobs, weary from their children's demands, weary from the stress of it all. And tomorrow they must start again.

Did Jesus Know Stress?

Jesus, too, strode this earth knowing the stress of ambiguity. Day after day he faced the training of his disciples (not always an easy or rewarding job), the presence of crowds of people, harassment from his enemies, and the scorn of leaders. We often see him seeking to get away, to find the quiet necessary for conversation with

God. For him, almost every moment of solitude had to be worked for, for almost three intense years.

How about your life? What kind of ambiguity do you live with and have you lived with for years and years? What is going on in your life that isn't resolving itself? Does this chapter, even though it may not have touched on your particular problem, help you to understand a little of why you might be feeling so very, very tired?

FOUR

High-stress Situations: When Life Wears You Down

When Sarah married Pete after his wife died, she looked forward to being a special kind of mother to his children, Dave and Sherrie. Sherrie accepted her right away; nine-year-old Dave did not. He hated her. He lied, refused to obey, yelled and screamed when she corrected him. In his teenage years his rebelliousness caused him to come after her with a butcher knife.

For seven years Sarah did everything she could think of to manage her stepson. Coping with him was the hardest thing she'd ever done. She called it the worst kind of emotional harassment. "If he'd been my own child," Sarah said, "I don't think it would have been so terrible. At least he wouldn't have been able to taunt me with the words, 'You're not my mother.' "

Sarah and I talked for a long time about the particular frustration of being a stepparent. "Too often," she admitted, "whether it's right or wrong, the success of your marriage seems to hang on whether you can get along with your stepchildren." The statistics for the breakup of marriages in which stepchildren are involved show how difficult such marriages are.

At first I thought Sarah's problem with her stepson would fit into the nonreciprocity category. But I began to see that this terrible kind of ongoing battle goes much deeper than the nonreciprocity issue. I then thought I would put it under high-ambiguity situations, those situations that don't resolve themselves. But when I really looked at the intensity on Sarah's face and heard in her voice the hurt and struggle of those painful years of trying to deal with hatred and rejection by a stepchild, I understood this to be one of the long-term agonies. Parents who must deal with these kinds of problems over a long period of time, especially with the success of their marriage hanging on the result, are in a high-stress situation.

Living Without Control

Women who have little or no control over their lives are in high-stress situations, too. A recent study by the National Institute for Occupational Safety and Health made in public treatment centers in Tennessee has documented some of the most stressful jobs. At the top of the list are health-care technicians, waitresses, and licensed practical nurses. (It must be noted that because of the location of this study [public treatment centers], people of higher-income jobs may not have been fairly represented, as they would be more likely to seek private treatment centers.)

People in these jobs are controlled by others — their

bosses, their patients, or customers. They are also controlled by the inefficiency of the system and/or time limits. This control is what makes their jobs stressful and, therefore, hazardous to their health.

There is not one study I know of that documents wives and mothers who have little or no control over their lives. There are many women controlled by alcoholic husbands, critical husbands, demanding husbands, or by patronizing husbands who control them with kindness in the same way a parent controls a precious only child.

There are also women who are controlled by their children. Five-year-old Monica comes to mind. Her father abandoned his family, and without him Monica's mother, Jean, cannot cope with her three young children. Monica has taken over the reigns. *She* decides what to eat and when. Jean fixes toast and catsup for breakfast because Monica has ordered it. Monica tells her mother to get up to take care of the baby. If Jean asserts herself, Monica screams until her mother gives in.

Monica orders, demands, controls. What will life be like for Monica and her mother in ten more years? Mothers who are controlled by domineering, temper-tantrum-throwing children are in high-stress situations.

Mothers who feel controlled by guilt are also in high-stress situations. Lorene, the mother of four young adults from ages nineteen to twenty-four, says her children are constantly calling for help. "Mom, I'll lose my job if you don't drive me." "Mom, if you don't help me clean my apartment, I'll lose my deposit." "Mom, if you don't lend me some money my fine will double." Lorene knows she meets too many of these unreasonable requests. She feels irritated at these demands but guilty when she doesn't meet them.

The Stresses of Parenthood

One of the greatest amounts of stress, the stress that saps our energy and leaves us feeling as if we'll never recover, comes to us through the lives of our children (even if we aren't stepparents).

When Christian mothers of teenagers and young adults get together and feel safe enough to speak honestly, they often bare their hearts over the pain they feel because their children are going their own way instead of God's way. The pain is especially great when these mothers have tried to do everything right.

Christian women rear their children convinced that if they do this and this and this, their children will glide through the rebellious years without incident. They work so hard, give so much, sacrifice to such an extent that they're certain their children will be the good ones.

Leah is a woman who "did it all" for her three children. She and her husband provided discipline, Christian teaching, Christian music, and a Christian community. Leah listened and nurtured and cooked and chauffeured. She arranged music lessons and camp sessions and family vacations. Today her children, ages eighteen to twenty-one, are all experimenting with drugs, alcohol, and sex. None of them are dating Christians or going regularly to church. Leah, always an energetic person, is feeling too tired to get out of bed in the morning. Her head aches and she has a strange biting pain that comes and goes in her neck and back.

Someone told her, "God was the perfect parent and look what happened to his children, Adam and Eve." She smiled, but it didn't take away the stress or the pain.

Ironically, stress over children's choices is not even on the stress charts (see pages 125-27 in the appendix). These charts don't mention the stress of bailing a son out of jail for drunk driving, the stress of a daughter moving in with a boyfriend, the stress of a beloved teenager turned stranger.

In time, many Christians learn to take these heart-breaks and turn their children over to God — a process that greatly deepens a parent's spiritual growth. But this process comes gradually for most people. In the meantime the stress and pain are very real.

Adults aren't the only ones under stress. The rate of suicide among teens reflects the pressures our youth are under. They're pressured to excel academically, socially, and athletically by parents, teachers, peers, and them-selves. Christian teenagers are expected to excel spiritu-ally as well.

Teens today are pressured into making moral judgments far earlier than any other generation, pressured into de-ciding their futures when they haven't even decided who they are. They're pressured into working to get a car and working to maintain a car. They're pressured into wearing the right jacket, the right shoes, the right hairstyle, and knowing the right music.

One of the big pressures is to get away from their parents' control, to be themselves, to be free — yet teens often need their parents at the same time. Add to this growing spurts and glandular changes, and it's easy to see why our teenagers hate to get out of bed in the morning. It's a good thing they're young; being a teenager is exhausting.

Few can even imagine the stress of heartbreak when parents learn their child is mentally or physically handicapped. The pain is so great that parents often reject the news at first because they're not equipped to handle it. Each of us thinks *our* child will be perfect and none of us are prepared for a different verdict. Marriages have fallen apart under this stress as couples blame each other because there's no one else to blame.

That's only the beginning. Following the news that a child is handicapped come months and years — a lifetime, really — of doctors, clinics, hospitals, special classes, special tutors, special equipment. Add to this your child's adjustment to a different kind of life. Priorities change rapidly when a handicapped child comes into the family. Lives and dreams and goals are all in upheaval. It takes all the energy a parent has. Many people in this situation eventually learn to draw on God's strength. That's good, but it's a process. It doesn't change the stressful reality that their lives are going to be forever different.

Yet, there is a time that is even more stressful. It's when a dreaded disease and/or death finds your child. A woman once said to me, "I would rather have my son dead than living in sin." That woman has never lost a child. She cannot comprehend what it means to know that she'll never see him come in the door again, to know that his children will never be.

When a parent must sit beside a stricken child, day after

day, sometimes month after month, and know that without a miracle the child will surely die, that parent begins to know real stress. That stress is magnified if well-meaning friends tell parents that increased faith in the Lord can make their child live.

Personal Problems

For many people, a real area of stress in life is lack of time alone. On Chinese junks (small marine vessels that house extended families), people have developed a strong rule whereby family members can say, "I'm going to the bow and while I'm there it is my space."

In our society we need to do essentially the same thing, but we often *don't* do it. Young women rushing between home, husband, the demands of small children, school, church work, and their jobs literally have no time for themselves. When they're exhausted they wonder why they're so resentful and why they laugh so little anymore. Only the strength of youth keeps them going.

Older women often balance the demands of teenagers, jobs, marriage, and elderly parents without the strength of youth. It's wearying. My friend Marilyn found herself with four generations — from baby granddaughter to her aged parents — living in her three-bedroom house. Even harder than caring for little children was caring for her mother. She writes:

> I realized that even though I was a grandmother myself, I still desired the approval of my mother; I did not want to hurt or disappoint her. . . . Mother's

> demands on my time were often picayune and excessive. She might call me from one end of the house in the midst of a difficult chore just to have me see a particular person in a soap opera. Or she might keep changing what she wanted for lunch even though I had it prepared. She would call me to cover her legs with her afghan, a task she was capable of doing for herself. No wonder I felt resentful and weary (Marilyn Fanning, *The Not-So-Golden Years*, Wheaton, IL: Victor Books, 1984).

One of the worst types of high-stress situations is marriage to an alcoholic. It means having a partner you can never count on, who humiliates you, drinks up all the money, and then blames you for his drinking. It may mean physical abuse and almost always mental abuse. It means fear for the children; it means pain in their lives. It means never being sure and never really counting on anything. It means dashed hopes and forgotten promises. It is the ultimate in stress just because it goes on and on.

Often women who lead overstressed lives find they must add the stress of their own alcohol/drug dependence to the already high level of stress. There is something terrible about knowing that what you are doing is wrong but doing it anyway. There's so much hiding, so much deceit, so much counter-planning so no one will know. Life becomes a macabre merry-go-round of stress that leads to addiction that leads to stress again.

If you know about such a situation, you can't close your eyes and think, *if only these women were Christians they wouldn't have these problems*. Our parishes house scores of hurting women ruled by drugs (including alcohol which *is* a drug). They are often skillfully adept at hiding their afflictions.

Anyone living in a situation he or she knows is wrong in the sight of God is living in a stressful situation. Kurt is a man whose life was entangled with a woman who was not his wife. Listen to the stress described:

> I am beginning to really hurt. I know I am believing Satan's lies because I really want to believe them. I know my relationship with Elaine is sin, sin in the eyes of God and in my own eyes. I know no matter how good my life looks, God's plan can never be totally fulfilled in my life as I am presently living it. But now it is not as simple to choose to obey God as it had been before. Now it is complicated by her feelings toward me, by my lies, by her job, by my emotions. There is no one I can talk to. Each day is filled with remorse. Each day is twenty-four hours of guilt.

There was no doubt about the stress in Kurt's life. Deliberately going against what God has said will cause terrible inner conflict.

Kurt's wife felt the stress of his infidelity in her life as well. When a woman discovers her husband in an unfaithful relationship, her world caves in. Everything she has given, worked toward, sacrificed for, suddenly seems to have no meaning. It feels as if her very life has ceased to count. Then the rejection hits. A woman who has measured her worth by her husband's love now feels worthless. Here is how one woman expressed herself as she sat across from me in a restaurant and poured out all the shame, hurt, and humiliation. Her tears splotched the tablecloth.

> It's all my fault. I'm no good. I know I must be sexually undesirable. My body's not beautiful like hers. I have nothing to offer. I'm no good to him. I don't think he ever loved me. I can look back and see that now. I've never really zinged him the way she did.

There's no way to measure the pain or the stress in this woman's life. There are so many women who have so many reasons to hurt, so many women who have good reason to feel tired.

Yet of all personal problems causing stress, the one that encompasses the greatest number of people is the problem of not enough money. Not having enough for the basic necessities such as food and warm clothing, year in and year out, is painful for everyone involved, especially for those women whose deepest instinct is to physically care for their families.

No money for recreation or vacations means that there is never a break or something to look forward to. No money for repairs means living with broken appliances, a leaky roof, an unreliable car. No money for the extra little things a mother wants for her children is, for some, the hardest of all. When a child is deprived, a mother feels that deprivation greatly.

For many, the hardest part of not ever having enough money is being dependent on others. My friend Deanna, whose husband just found a job after a long, long stretch, said that depending on the Christian community for so much help was humbling. "It was probably good for me, but it caused me so much anxiety."

Stress Caused by Work

There are many professions in which high-stress situations come with the territory. A friend spent months being both hostess and nurse to her sister-in-law who had burned out from her job as a welfare worker. Her sister-in-law's words were: "I just can't bear any more of the problems of destitute people."

It is no big surprise that my friend grew weary from the strain of nursing this sister-in-law. As I said before, people in health care are at the top of the list when it comes to stressful work. So are fire fighters, policemen, teachers, and particularly Christian ministry workers.

If your daily work touches crisis-wrought people, that may well be the reason you feel so very weary.

On the other hand, it's possible that the stress you feel may be something you're doing to yourself. People who are overscheduled are their own worst enemy. Before I ran out of energy and had to revamp my lifestyle, there was a little song that I hummed to myself all day long:

I have to hurry,
    I have to get this done.
I have to be there in ten minutes,
    I'm going to have to run.

The song had no ending because, even though I knew better, as soon as I had one item clicked off my schedule I was nearly late for the next. One Christian author put it this way:

> The temptation to overwork is potentially one of the greatest problems for dedicated, sincere Christians today. We are more often characterized by frantic activity, fatigue, and weariness than love, compassion, and joy. (Tim Hansel, *When I Relax I Feel Guilty,* Elgin, IL: David C. Cook Publishing, 1979.)

People tell us over-scheduled Christians to slow down, but we are often running a race that is hard to get out of. I would say, "As soon as I get to the top of that hill over there I'll rest." Then I'd say, "Well, maybe just the next hill." When I got *there* I'd push a little more until I reached a further hill. We'll talk later about what motivates the over-scheduled person and how to change before you fall apart. But for now, it's enough to say that an over-scheduled life is a stressful and exhausting way to live.

One type of stressful lifestyle and one that we're seeing more of today comes when a wife becomes more celebrated in her career, in terms of either fame or money, than her husband.

It was something we were used to seeing in movie stars and seemed usually to precipitate those divorces for which Hollywood became famous. Now we have women physicians, anchorwomen on the nightly news, executives, and scores of other top-salary positions for professional women. Trying to compensate for her husband's ego and pretending at home that she is not successful when she is causes many women to lead double lives. That causes greater stress than facing the facts and trying to work through the situation.

Troubles in the Church

Church activity conflicts can cause end-of-your-rope weariness for everyone involved. Sisters, laypeople, priests — all Christian ministry workers for that matter — come into a new church or organization with hopes held high.

I remember Father Langley who asked for the hard parish that no one else would take. He knew with God's help he could lead this church into becoming a godly faith community.

The parish loved him . . . at first. But he took a hard stand on some issues; such a hard stand that the council members eventually chose sides and wouldn't budge. This carried over into other council decisions.

Father Langley, who had always dreaded out-and-out conflicts, was now in the middle of several. This sort of breach wasn't what he'd hoped or planned for at all. He developed an annoying pain in his stomach that was always worse just before and after the council meetings.

Then those who were "on his side" asked him to be the chaplain for a growing interdenominational group of married couples. This group appreciated Father Langley, loved him, and showered him with affection. It was the reciprocity issue; in return for appreciation he gave the group his love, his very life.

Now the other council members really had something to complain about. ''Who pays his salary,'' they demanded, ''their churches or ours?'' Eventually many of the council members began experiencing pains similar to Father Langley's. They saw the issue very clearly *their* way. Father Langley wasn't giving the church his full support as he was supposed to do. They like him as a person but . . . well, it just wasn't right.

One man was so upset he left the church and hasn't come back. Yet the issue at hand loomed more important than reconciliation. In the end, Father Langley left the parish he'd once pastored with such high hopes. He needed to rest. He was worn out from five long years of stress. The council members, their high hopes also having fallen short, watched him go with saddened hearts.

If this kind of conflict, either as a pastor or a church member, is in your life, you may have the answer as to why all the energy and enthusiasm you used to have so much of has now faded and disappeared. Conflict is the great thief of energy.

Spiritual Failures

''Why can't you be quiet like Susie?''

''Why can't you stay clean like Mary?''

When we were little our mothers may have solicited our cooperation by comparing us to the good little girls. Now that we're adults we, ourselves, continue with the comparisons. We judge ourselves — our intrinsic worth, our achievements, our spiritual progress — by what others have done or are doing. When the burned-out Christian woman compares herself to others, she rarely gives herself the credit she deserves. There is always someone who prays better, studies more, reads the Bible longer — someone who is more patient, more pleasant, and more together than she will ever be.

If you really want to succeed spiritually (and who doesn't want to be a success in life as a Christian?), the stress of never measuring up, never being good enough, can be exhausting.

The good news is, it's all right to be weak so that Jesus can be your strength; it's all right to be imperfect because Jesus is the only perfect one. Jesus died on the Cross for *everyone's* sins, not everyone's but yours.

We want to be proud of ourselves and make the ones who love us proud. This pursuit only adds to our pain. What do we do about it? We'll discuss this later on in the book. For now, if you are really, really tired from not measuring up, you are not alone. On all sides, weary, imperfect Christians feel the same as you do.

What kind of high-stress situation are you in? Maybe it hasn't been mentioned here. Even so, do you have a good idea of why you're feeling so weary?

FIVE

Difficult Transitions: Why Change Is Never Easy

My friend Julie, a writer, was fifty pounds overweight. Although still young, she wore out-of-date clothing styles and tucked her hair in a little-old-lady bun. Her smile showed a chipped, uneven front tooth. She was so unsure of herself she hid at home behind the mask of ''I'm a writer, I need solitude.''

Then one day she had the tooth repaired. She was filled with new confidence at every smile. Next she shed the extra pounds and bought a high fashion outfit. Encouraged by friends, she began to teach a class for writers.

Julie felt excitement over her new image, but her husband didn't share that excitement. He'd felt happier when she was overweight and he began to make critical comments about her new look. Even so, Julie took another plunge and had her hair cut and permed. Even she was stunned over the person who smiled back at her from the mirror. Was she going to like this new creation? It was such a change she had trouble getting used to her new self.

Her husband found it too much to handle. He'd been secure when she was overweight and hidden at home. In time he packed his bags and moved out.

Changes are so difficult that when change does come, physical and mental energies are drained away. In the above story, Julie's self-image was so altered by her weight loss and then her husband's leaving that her life was in upheaval for over two years. She was not alone; all of us feel stress and energy loss when we have to make or are forced to make a difficult transition.

Changing Lifestyles

Benjamin Franklin once said that fish and houseguests have one thing in common: After three days they both stink. What I hear him saying is this: Even one extra person living in your household long enough to upset the routine becomes a burden. Change rarely feels good. It gets to be like a piece of hair from a haircut that sticks in the back of your collar; it irritates.

One of the most familiar changes, and one that is bound to have its irritating moments, occurs when people make the transition from single life to married life. Even if you are one-hundred-percent happy with your new spouse, you still have an adjustment to make.

Whether you realize it or not, your life before you were married had developed a pattern. You had a set time for meals, a certain way you did or didn't hang your clothes, and special television programs you always watched. Now, happy though you are, meals are different, the clothes closet is not the way you like it, and your television schedule isn't the same anymore. What's more, you've always liked sitting in the front of the church and he wants to sit in the back. You don't exercise in the same way in the same place, your towel isn't where you left it, and you've never in your life slept with the bedroom window wide open. His parents keep coming over uninvited. He wastes money and then asks you to be more careful with your spending. He's late and doesn't call. You're late and you resent having to call. You thought sex was always going to be so wonderful and it sometimes isn't.

You feel irritated and really tired. That's a pretty normal response. Your body actually feels it when there is a change in routine. The change from singleness to being married takes effort, sweat, and energy. Even though the transition may be difficult, it doesn't last forever. It's like crossing a rope bridge over a deep canyon. Once you get to the other side, the worst is over.

An even scarier transition than marriage is remarriage after having had one marriage fail. You've been through so much that now, more than anything else, you want this marriage to work.

The remarried woman asks herself, *Is he really Mr. Wonderful? If he's not, am I going to blow it? Is he going to love me when he sees my imperfections up close?* If your first husband walked out on you, the doubts about the future hang on for a long time. These worrisome thoughts come with the transition. Everybody feels nervous crossing a canyon on a rope bridge.

Once the transition into marriage is made, the next transition period is foreseeable. There's nothing like a new baby to throw a smoothly flowing life into upheaval.

When babies come, they take over. They create mountains of work for weary parents and demand that everyone revolve themselves around their schedule.

Our young friends couldn't have awaited their baby's arrival with more anticipation. They could hardly wait for little Joel to be born. After a very short while the new mother called her mother. "Oh, Mom," she sobbed, the tears falling, "I didn't know a baby was going to be so much work."

A new baby is an incredibly difficult transition. Even though having a child is worth it all a thousand times over, that doesn't cease to make it hard. For me (I had my first eight in twelve years), the hardest part was finding out I was pregnant again.

"Bill, I'm a day late," I'd alert him. Then the wait would begin. In those days there was no easy pregnancy test, just the time-honored way of waiting for the next month to roll around. (You could pay $7.50 for a rabbit test but we never had $7.50 to spare.) Each day dragged because I wanted so much to know.

Agonizing as the wait was, by the time one day after another pointed to another pregnancy, I'd had plenty of time to make the adjustment. I'd planned where the new crib would go, how we'd rearrange the existing children's beds and how we'd once more surprise the grandmothers. Fortunately we lived in a neighborhood where big families abounded and a new baby was always welcome.

Never let it be said it was a piece of cake, though. No matter how many times you go through it, a new baby means a transition, and transitions are never easy.

The Workplace

If there were any words I dreaded hearing from Bill those first years of our marriage they were, "I think I'm going to look for a new job." Even though I wanted his career to advance, I knew what a new job meant. He'd be crabby and preoccupied. He'd withdraw from me and be inconsistent with the children. He'd wear a frown all evening and a scowl all weekend.

At first I didn't know how to handle this kind of change in Bill, and I felt really hurt. But in time, although I didn't know that the word for it was *transition,* I came to realize that until Bill felt safe in his new job, this was the way it was going to be.

Now as I reflect on those days, I wonder if Bill was that way on the outside, what must he have been like on the inside? I can imagine his doubts. *What if I make the step and can't handle it? What if the man who hired me is disappointed? What if I can't figure it all out?*

These doubts, only a few of the hundreds that people feel in starting a new job, are only the beginning. There's the work itself. It's hard. It's often complicated, especially in today's electronic age. There seems to be too much to learn, too many people to satisfy, too many instructions. Add to this the body's possible reactions — backache, headache, and stomachache.

Getting adjusted to a new job can be far more trepidating than crossing a rope bridge because so much depends on it — ego, self-worth, livelihood, the future. It's more like getting across a canyon on a tightrope.

Is there anything worse than starting a new job?

Yes, losing the job you have. Those words in a boss' office, "I'm sorry . . ."; or that notice in a pay envelope, "This is to inform you . . ." — both feel like rejection.

Losing a job is like hearing that your parents never wanted you, that your spouse doesn't love you, or that your children don't need you. It's the worst kind of criticism. When a friend says, "Cheer up, this isn't the end of the world," it only makes it worse because obviously this friend doesn't understand the hollowness in the pit of your stomach or the lump in your throat or the pressure in your chest.

Losing a job and having to start all over is a transition that's worse than crossing a canyon on a tightrope. It's like having to cross a canyon with a mighty leap when you feel less like Superlady than you've ever felt before.

Suffering Saints

A man swinging an ax or a golf club is suddenly stopped by a heart attack. A woman racing to a meeting doubles over when the blinding pain of a brain tumor halts her life. Families going along concerned with baseball scores and next summer's vacations find their priorities totally reversed when one of their members receives the dreaded news of cancer.

These kinds of stressful transitions are lifestyle changing. Nothing is ever the same again, and the adjustments are fierce. Losing your sight or hearing or the ability to walk means an enormous change in living, working, friends, travel, leisure, even food, as shopping and cooking become a major chore.

Millions of people live with pain. Chronic back pain alone affects 23 million Americans. Another 21 million suffer daily from arthritis. Thirty-six million have migraine headaches, and an ever-increasing number must endure the unrelenting pain of cancer. A life in which chronic pain replaces health is a transition that no one without pain can comprehend.

Often forgotten are the ones who love the afflicted and must also make a lifestyle transition into the world of caring for the sick. For each of the millions who live with pain and sickness there are also millions more whose lives have also become forever different as they care for the sick.

Auntie Dee Dee comes to mind. Not my real aunt, she and Mother became close friends in the 1920's when they were both young missionaries in the Chinese church in Seattle. Then Auntie Dee Dee went on to the Chinese church in San Francisco's famous Chinatown. She gave that church her life. She loved the giving. She crisscrossed the Chinatown hillsides in wind and rain or searing sun, meeting people, inviting them to church, helping in their crises, teaching their children. In return she was loved deeply and revered by the people she called her own.

The years fled by and soon it was time for Auntie Dee Dee to retire. She chose a whole new lifestyle. She would have her own little apartment in a retirement home in Kalamazoo, close to her sister Dorothy. She was looking forward to it. The two sisters would have such a good time. They did — for a while.

Then Dorothy became progressively ill with Alzheimer's disease. Auntie Dee Dee became full-time nurse until her whole life, even her letters, became concerned with whether Dorothy had a good day or not.

Mother and I talked about Auntie Dee Dee one day as we read her letter. "Isn't it too bad?" we said. Yet in my heart I know Auntie Dee Dee, whose love for Jesus and all people is her hallmark, finds joy in a life that allows her to minister, even though she is eighty years old.

But in no way am I naïve enough to think it's easy. The transition into the world of sickness and pain, either as a patient or caregiver, is long, hard, tedious, and seldom fully appreciated.

Mid-life Crisis

Today we hear and read so much about "mid-life crisis" that we're not so surprised when we see a good marriage of twenty-five or more years floundering; or see a stable forty-year-old family man make a foolish decision; or meet a woman who can't, for now, bear her family.

We all know people who are in an age-related crisis. For some it's the crisis of passing into middle age in a culture geared to youth. For others it's the realization that the dreams and goals of yesterday are never going to be fully realized. For many it's just a sense of futility because there seem to be such unsatisfactory answers to the questions of life.

If you or someone you love is having a hard time facing another birthday — or even another day — be gentle on yourself or your friend. This is a rocky time. It may feel like you've slipped off the rope bridge and landed in the canyon flood below . . . with the worst part being that you're still alive.

Death and Divorce

Terri Hicks opened her eyes and saw that it was just barely morning. Sitting on the bed, her husband, police detective Sam Hicks, was pulling on his trousers. "Where are you going?" she questioned sleepily. "You don't have to be at work until afternoon."

"I know," Sam answered, "but I'm going to question a witness from that murder case. Pray for me. This guy's a bad one." He tucked in his shirt and strapped on his revolver.

Terri watched him run a comb through his hair. "Be careful, honey."

He leaned over the bed and kissed her good-bye. "See you tonight."

Four hours later Sam Hicks was dead. A bullet from the fugitive's rifle had ended his young life.

For Terri, his widow, the terrible transition had begun. In losing Sam, everything changed. She went from being cared for to aloneness. From companionship to aloneness. From physical pleasure to aloneness.

Her teenagers did things they wouldn't have done if Sam were alive. Her friends and family took advantage of her in ways they wouldn't have dared if Sam had had his say.

She went from always considering Sam's needs to not having to consider them at all; from cooking his favorite foods to not having anyone really appreciate her efforts; from depending on his judgment to often not knowing what to do.

There were changes in finances, changes in friendship patterns, changes in established routines. Because they had shared a life of prayer and ministry, the changes in Terri's spiritual life were enormous. She went from trusting God to look out for Sam to anger at God to wondering if God actually existed.

When discussing the stress that wipes out our energies, it's safe to say that the death of a loved one is the greatest stress of all.

Yet there are others whose loss, although not through death, feels just as final. These are the many women whose marriages end in divorce. My friend Joanne says that, to her, Terri is one of the fortunate ones. Terri is a widow, yes, but a widow whose husband had loved her. Terri is alone, yes, but she had the support, not the suspicion, of the entire community. She is alone, yes, but she does not have to make excuses.

Even though death rates 100, at the very top of the stress chart (see the appendix), and divorce is next with a rating of 73, there are many who believe that life after divorce is harder to bear. Too often the church and the community are unsupportive, even condemning; or worse, apathetic, thus rejecting further someone who has already been rejected.

If you and your husband divorce, the transitions, especially if there are children, are many and painful and complicated.

There are changes in the way you feel about yourself, often not very good at first, especially if there has been a lot of humiliation — change in the children's lives, change in housing, change in responsibilities.

There's the loss of his income, his friends, his family, his intimacy. Even if he was impossible, even if living away from him seems better than living with him, that doesn't alter the fact that getting on with life means many new adjustments.

One friend, even though her husband was unfaithful from the beginning of their marriage and had threatened her life, says that she has been five years getting over the sense of loss that her divorce caused.

Sometimes divorce means losing a child. Going from twenty-four hours a day caring for a child to not knowing where he is, or what she's eating, or if his homework is done, or if she's happy, rips apart a mother's heart. Often she bears this pain alone because it's too painful to share or because people don't know enough to reach out to her.

Those who haven't been divorced tend to take divorce in stride. "Oh, that's too bad," they say, and continue on without realizing or understanding the pain of the divorced person or the long period of stress ahead.

The Christian Facade

Since no one's life is free of difficult transitions, no one has a life that is all smooth sailing. So often we Christians hate to admit that we may be going through sorrow or grief or tough times. It sounds so unbrave or unsuper or unchristian to shed tears or dread tomorrow.

Christians going through hard times can think, *How silly of me, how overly pious I get*. We have only to look at Jesus to see there is nothing wrong in crying when the stress is overwhelming.

Picture him in an olive grove, on his knees in prayer. His friends are scattered about but they are asleep. All alone he faces the most agonizing transition of his earthly life. Beads of sweat form on his brow. Then as the stress of the situation worsens, the sweat beads become like drops of blood. We hear his cry, "Father, I don't want to have to suffer. . . ." He was so much like us.

Yet he had to suffer and so do we at times. There is suffering in life that can't be escaped; we all have to go through it.

There is something we can do when we are suffering, when we are sidetracked with weariness, when we are overstressed; something we can *do* about the tensions in our lives.

The next chapters are about *you* — chemically, spiritually, mentally, physically. They are going to help you. If the following principles are applied you'll probably find that you *aren't* so tired, that you *have* the energy you need every day.

SIX
Our Bodies Under Stress and How We Avoid the Symptoms

I sat back in a comfortable chair beside the pool and closed my eyes. I'd been swimming and completed two laps, which was all I ever had the stamina for, and now I was ready to work on my tan. A soft inner voice nudged me, "Sit up and watch the children."

I sat up and looked for eight-year-old Catrina, my neighbor. She was fine. The inner voice spoke again. "Look for Nene." Nene, another neighbor, was twelve and big for her age. Even so, I couldn't see her.

Was that her over there under the water? Why were her arms waving in such an awkward way? Was she swimming? Her head popped out of the water and she looked right into my eyes with a desperate, horrible look. She gasped and sank beneath the surface of the pool.

I looked for something to throw to her. There were no life preservers hanging on the wall. I looked for help. The lifeguard wasn't there. "Nene's drowning!" I yelled to my friend Virginia as I jumped into the pool. I thought I could get her by the hand and pull her to safety.

Under the water Nene saw me coming. In her desperation she threw her arms and legs around me and hung on. But she weighs more than I do and the force of her weight pulled us both under. With my arms pinned down I couldn't help her and we were going deeper. Too late, I realized my mistake. I could feel the water rushing around us as we sank tangled together to the bottom. I normally panic at being under water for even a second, but in this case I was incredibly clearheaded. Then I heard that inner voice again. It said, "Push her."

I gave Nene a mighty shove that untangled us. Even though I could feel myself rising to the top, a terrible helplessness tore at me. Nene was on the bottom and I didn't know how to save her. Surfacing, I gasped for air. "Help!" It seemed to take all the oxygen I had left to call those words. Virginia jumped in, clothes and all.

Then, to my utter surprise, I saw Nene safe at the edge of the pool. My forceful shove had pushed her in such a way that she had come up in just the right place for her friend to grasp her hand and pull her to safety.

Nene was safe, I was safe. Virginia had gotten wet for nothing. We stood around the pool and laughed, and hugged Nene in relief.

Then Virginia suggested that as long as she was soaking wet we might as well swim. We swam one lap, two, three, four . . . ten, eleven, twelve. I kept waiting to get tired. We swam some more. I'd never swum so well. *Why?* I wondered. Then it occurred to me: it was adrenaline. Adrenaline had poured into my system and was giving me all sorts of extra energy.

From the moment I'd perceived Nene's situation, my

whole body had responded to her rescue. Adrenaline and noradrenaline had equipped me for emergency action. I first felt their effects on my cardiovascular system. They constricted my arteries and made my heart beat faster in order to rush more blood to my muscles and brain. They drew my blood back from my skin and also quickened its clotting time so I would bleed less if injured. To fight possible infection, they raised my white blood count.

They also took action to speed up my metabolism. They increased my red blood count, delivering more oxygen to my cells so I could burn my fuel faster; they increased my supply of fuel itself by stimulating my liver and muscles to release sugar into my blood. When this happened my pancreas measured the rise in my blood sugar and began pouring insulin into the blood to enable the sugar to enter my cells.

In addition to my cardiovascular system and the endocrine glands being supremely involved in this rescue, my digestive system slowed or stopped completely in order to divert all available energy to the present need.

With this kind of physical reaction taking place I had more energy and ability than I could ever remember having. I don't know how long I could have gone on swimming that day. I had, it seemed, a hundred times my normal ability.

The release of adrenaline into our bodies in times of stress only emphasizes how marvelously and wonderfully we are made.

Going home that day I said to myself, "You're probably going to cry over this before the day is out, but that's OK." (I remember losing a child at the beach and being so calm all the time he was lost. It wasn't until he was safe in bed that night that I burst into tears.) To my surprise the tears over Nene's rescue never came. I realized later that the swimming had replaced tears as the usual body-system letdown that follows a crisis.

Now let's look at another situation: Picture yourself outside on a dark night. You have two more blocks to walk before reaching your parked car. Suddenly you hear footsteps behind you . . . gaining on you.

The sound of those footsteps sends an immediate message to the adrenal glands. Your heart starts thumping (supplying more oxygen to the cells). You start to run. The footsteps behind you speed up. You start running faster; you didn't know you could run so fast.

This is not a foot race at a picnic. All the parts of your body — the liver, pancreas, heart, digestive system, the whole endocrine system — have teamed up to give you maximum speed for your flight. You get to your car, slam the door and lock it just in time to see a man with a mask over his face run by you.

Whew! You're OK. Shaking, you start home. Halfway there tears of relief begin to fall. At home you tell your family all about your escape and the tears come again. Next you call your sister or a friend and tell her. Crying and talking (and laughter) are like my swimming all those laps. They're a good way of dealing with the effects of the adrenaline that courses through your body in times of crisis.

Now let's say that the next night the same thing happens. What kind of an emotional state would you be in? I hope your answer is "Terrible." I hope nobody answers, "I'm a Christian. I wouldn't be upset."

Your body and emotions have been on a seesaw. Your heart has speeded up, your whole sugar function is topsy-turvy, your digestive system from swallowing to elimination has been tampered with. Your sleep has probably been affected. You may be irritable, over-hungry, light-headed, weepy, and constipated (except for when you have diarrhea).

It's very likely that you don't feel well at all. You call work and tell them you just can't come in or you call your mother and ask her if she can watch the baby so you can take a nap.

You probably tell yourself something like, "I've been through a lot. I'm going to give myself some rest, a few days off, a bubble bath, and dinner out tonight."

Your family is equally sympathetic because you've been through something quite terrible. Of course you pray. You ask God to take away the fear. You thank him for your safety. You forgive your would-be assailant. In time you get better. You hope you've learned not to walk on dark streets alone.

Your body and your emotions have survived a stressful situation.

Invent a Family

The family you are about to meet is not a real-life family, but perhaps you may be able to identify with some of the stressful situations they experience.

George and Jane have been married almost fifteen years. When you see them sitting in their pew at church with sixteen-year-old Amy and fourteen-year-old Tim you probably think what a happy family they must be. Amy looks like such a lovely teenager and Tim, looking so confident, is wearing the latest "in" jacket. Jane, who operates a word processor for a mailing depot, is a little heavier than she was last year, but she is always dressed to perfection, each blond hair perfectly in place. George, a shop supervisor for a crane company, has that tall, muscular, all-American look.

They all look as though they are intent on the sermon. Actually, none is listening; there's just too much else on their minds.

Tim is deeply concerned about the new school he started going to last week. He hates the new neighborhood and wishes they hadn't moved. He wishes he knew some of the other kids. He wishes he were three inches taller so he could try out for basketball. He shoves his hands in the pockets of his new jacket. The soft lining feels good, like his blanket when he was little. He wishes his parents hadn't made such a big deal about how much the jacket cost. Sometimes he just can't stand his family.

Amy is still remembering the angry words she had with her mother, actually her stepmother. Her own mother died when she was a baby. Being a stepchild didn't bother her at all when she was young; she never even thought about it. But she sure did now. Every time Jane (as Amy calls her in her mind) complains, Amy silently answers back, "So what? You're not my *real* mother, anyway." The fight at dinner had been over the beef stew. Amy thinks she'd asked a perfectly legitimate question — "Why do you always have to make beef stew on Saturdays? I hate beef stew." Then she'd added, "You make it because I hate it. I know you do."

Jane had gotten so angry that Amy had rather enjoyed herself. The look on her father's face was also enjoyable. He didn't say a word but she knew he felt sorry for her.

George's mind wasn't on the children at all. He was thinking of Betsy. Sweet, twenty-two-year-old Betsy who works in the company office. Part of him said to forget her; another part of him didn't want to. Their clandestine relationship had gone pretty far. She was there every day . . . laughing, fun, lighthearted. She made him feel young. Jane had asked him about Betsy after the company picnic but he'd denied everything. The trouble was that Jane was getting more and more irritable. Also, she constantly complained about money. She wanted them to live on a strict budget. He couldn't live that way, especially now.

Jane didn't even realize she was massaging her shoulders while she sat there. They'd been tense and tight for so long now that she was almost used to it. Quietly she reached down for her purse and slid her hand inside for a Tums. Lately her stomach had been constantly upset.

She thought about the trouble last night at dinner with Amy. She thought she'd handled it all wrong. She shouldn't have blown up. It was just that Amy was so critical of everything. She wished George would support her when it came to Amy. It seemed like neither Amy nor George appreciated her at all.

She looked across the church at a woman listening

carefully to the sermon. Jane envied the woman's seeming closeness to God. Lately Jane felt she hardly knew God. She wished she had prayed more before they bought the new house. Maybe if she had, they wouldn't have made such a mistake. There were so many things wrong with it and now they were stuck. The payments meant there was no way she could quit her job.

She'd been on that job only a month and already hated it as much as she hated anything. She sighed, almost out loud. Questions about the future swirled around in her mind but she just couldn't face the answers right now.

She let her thoughts center where they always ended up centering anyway, on George. She'd known there was someone else even before she'd seen those looks between him and Betsy at the picnic. Jane's heart literally ached when she thought of how far apart she and George had become. Yet she loved him. Ironic. She'd once told her mother she'd never love an unfaithful husband.

Of course the thing with Betsy only made the money problem worse. Their finances were totally out of control. Despite their combined salaries, creditors constantly called about missed payments. She had no idea how much George was spending on his mistress. Money had always slid through George's fingers anyway, even when he hadn't been spending it on some girl.

Jane looked at her watch. Would the sermon never end? She needed to get home. She pulled awkwardly on her dress that was too tight. It was the only decent dress she had that she could fit into. What with the new job, new house, the trouble with George, and everything else, she'd gained twenty pounds. She hated to walk by a mirror.

Jane felt like crying. She just wanted to sit there and let the tears flow, but of course she couldn't. What would people think? She knew everyone regarded them as a "together" family. Besides, she was a Christian. If she really believed she could do all things through Christ, then there was no need to cry.

To us, it's obvious that Jane is trying to deal with too many stressful situations. However Jane doesn't see it that way. She thinks, *I've always handled things. I can handle this*. What she doesn't understand is that when her fears were confirmed at the picnic, when Amy falsely accused her last night, her whole body responded to what was happening. Just as the body of the woman who was followed on a dark night went into high gear so she could flee her assailant, Jane's body has done the very same thing to help her fight her crises.

Heart, muscles, pancreas, liver, digestive system, the whole endocrine system — all went into action. The woman who was nearly attacked ended up crying as her body system let down. After I jumped in to rescue Nene I was able to swim off the extra adrenaline. Jane isn't able to understand that she has faced the same adrenaline-producing conflicts and that she needs to allow herself to let down. Also, she needs to be kind to herself and her body. Instead, her neck and shoulders ache. Her stomach and chest hurt. She's over-hungry and she explodes at Amy.

After church she went home feeling so lightheaded and dizzy all she wanted to do was lie down. The woman who had almost been mugged did that. Jane did not. What Jane *did* was busy herself in the kitchen because she *always* fixes a big dinner on Sundays. Beforehand, though, she had slipped into the bathroom and swallowed a tranquilizer. As she'd opened the bottle she'd thought of Darlene, her friend at church. She was sure Darlene would never take a tranquilizer. Darlene was too good a Christian. Jane was already feeling like a failure as a wife and mother. Now she felt like a failure as a Christian, too.

Later that afternoon someone from the church called. Would Jane be in charge of the Friday night potlucks for the next month? "No, no, no," Jane thought, "I can hardly get through the day." She told the caller she'd be glad to be in charge. In the back of her mind she gave herself ten extra points on God's "scorecard." It was sort of like doing extra credit when you think you've failed a test.

On Monday morning Jane ate half a doughnut and drank two cups of coffee in between getting the family off to work and school. She was really hungry and she would have eaten more except for her weight. She raced through the house making beds, picking things up, and cleaning the kitchen. "Just leave it," one of her friends said, but she couldn't. She couldn't ask Amy or Tim to do it either because neither one of them cleaned up thoroughly. Jane often told herself that she couldn't help it that she liked things done right.

That night before Jane dashed out the door to Bible study class at Darlene's, Amy came stomping into the kitchen. "You've shrunk my sweater," she accused. "You weren't supposed to wash it in the machine."

"You're the one that threw it in the dirty clothes."

"It says *hand* wash," Amy yelled. "Why don't you read the directions?"

Jane yelled back, "I don't have time to read directions."

Amy glared at her stepmother. "You *never* have time," she said.

"Shut up, Amy. You have no idea how hard I try."

Jane's heart was still pounding when she pulled into Darlene's driveway.

That night when Darlene asked if anyone needed prayer, Jane raised her hand. "I do," she admitted. For months she'd needed prayer but this was the first time she'd let anyone know.

"Can you tell us about it?"

"Well, it's just that I'm so tired. . . . " She couldn't mention George, that wasn't fair. She couldn't admit how she'd screamed at Amy. Someone had already told her how wonderful she was to do the Friday potlucks; she couldn't admit that was a mistake. So she said, "My job tires me out."

The women gathered around her and prayed that she wouldn't be so weary. Theirs were sweet, confident prayers that asked God's blessing on her life, her family, and her health.

"Thank you." Jane smiled at the women. "I really do feel better."

"You're healed," Darlene promised. "I know you're healed of your weariness."

The next evening George didn't come home for dinner nor did he call. Amy was still sulking from the skirmish the night before and Tim complained about the dinner.

Even before the meal was over, the terrible weariness came back. She wanted to make some calls about the potluck that evening but she was too tired.

In the bathroom mirror she accused herself. "Some Christian you are! Your friends pray for you — and, if anything, you're worse. Where's your faith?" She wished she'd never admitted she needed prayer.

On Wednesday she left work early. There was something wrong with her and she thought if she could just get home and sleep for a while she'd be fine. She lay on the sofa and closed her eyes. She was barely asleep when the phone rang. It was the manager of the discount store. Tim was in his office; he'd been caught shoplifting. Jane was instantly awake. Her heart raced all the way to the store. What would she say? How could Tim have done something like that?

At dinner she could hardly swallow. Twice she raced to the bathroom with sudden diarrhea. The phone rang again. Someone had forgotten to tell her there was a meeting at the church tonight to discuss the potluck dinner. Jane hung up the phone, appalled that she'd agreed to come. She knew she should stay home but she hated letting people down when she'd said she'd do something. Her whole body felt strange.

At the meeting she sometimes couldn't follow what was being said. On the way home she felt tears falling down her cheeks. "Stop it," she commanded herself. "Crying isn't going to help."

At home, George glared at her. "Did you know I had to go up to Amy's school today?"

"What for?"

"Someone reported her for smoking in the girls' room."

Jane sat down. "Amy? Oh, George, what are we going to do? First Tim and now Amy."

"It's not their fault."

"What do you mean by that?"

"Face it, you're the one who's at fault. You yell at Amy. You run off in the evening to Bible study or the church. The kids don't know where to turn."

Hot anger welled up inside her. She could feel the heat moving up her body, through her neck, and into her head. She was furious. She wanted to scream, to hit him, to hurt him. She struggled for control. Darlene flashed before her eyes. Darlene would never scream at or hit her husband. With extraordinary effort Jane walked out of the room.

The following Monday, under questioning at Scripture study, Jane admitted she didn't feel well. "Maybe it's sin," someone said. The women gathered around her and prayed that Jane would recognize any sin in her life that had caused her to feel so alienated from God. "You're going to feel better," Darlene promised again, adding, "Did you consider going to confession?" Jane hadn't been to confession in over a year. Yes, maybe she should have, but there was never the time. Maybe sin was the problem.

Two days later Jane was seated in the doctor's office. The diarrhea was much worse and now she could hardly breathe. "I just want to cry," she said.

The doctor had known Jane for a long time and said, "Why don't you? It would be all right, you know."

The kindness and the lack of expectations from this old

friend overwhelmed her. Jane put her head on the doctor's desk and sobbed and sobbed and sobbed.

As you read about Jane did you find some similarities between her life and yours? Are the lack of appreciation and the unsolvable problems, the high-stress situations and the difficult transitions of your life getting to you, too? Are you feeling some physical stress symptoms? Are you praying and finding it doesn't help as much as it should? Do you still clean the house and go to meetings even when you're exhausted? Is your family the kind that would be sympathetic if you were almost mugged but doesn't even notice when you're falling apart from too much stress? Do you want to cry and cry and cry?

If you answered yes to these questions, you stand alongside a vast crowd of good and wonderful women. Whenever I talk to women about stress and the resulting weariness in their lives, tears fall. When I say it's not as much a spiritual problem as they think — that their physical bodies are simply overloaded — even more tears fall.

Everyone asks the same questions: "What can I do? How can I get over feeling this way?" I understand just how you feel and there *are* some answers here for you.

SEVEN
Creating a New Lifestyle

A woman was going down the road of life when she fell into the hands of stressors. They robbed her of her energy, wounded her, and left her totally exhausted.

A priest saw her lying there all weary and out of energy and said, "This poor woman has a spiritual problem. I'll remember to pray for her at church."

Then a Levite came by and said, "This woman really looks all worn out but I know she can get up if she wants to. After all, 'Where there's a will there's a way.' "

Next a Samaritan came by and saw how badly wounded and exhausted the woman was. This Samaritan canceled all her plans and bandaged the wounds of the woman lying there, pouring on the oil of compassion and the wine of nurturing. Then she saw to it that the woman had a place where she could rest and said that whatever it cost to see her well again she would spend.

Jesus asked which of these was a neighbor to the woman who had fallen into the hands of stressors.

The listeners replied, "The one who had mercy."

Jesus said, "Go and do likewise." (See Luke 10:25-37.)

When you see yourself as an exhausted victim of too much stress, then you know that Jesus would have you stop in the middle of your journey, care for your wounds, and rest until you are better. For a season of your life you must be a Good Samaritan to yourself.

Being Your Own Good Samaritan

The house was overrun with children from ages eight to twelve. All of them were planning to spend the night. The evening was hot, the day had been busy. Now the children, Patrick's guests, had commandeered the bathroom, the kitchen, and the living room. I felt I couldn't stand their noise or clutter any longer. I literally walked out on them.

It was a perfect night for a walk and without a word I left them all to find their own towels, make their own popcorn, cook their own hot dogs, and figure out their own sleeping arrangements.

A scarlet sunset shimmered in the evening sky and within half a mile I began to feel completely calm. As I walked, I began to reflect a little on the words of Jesus who said, "Whoever wishes to save his life will lose it, but whoever loses his life for my sake will find it" (Matthew 16:25). I'd always taken this to mean that for the sake of others I was to do what had to be done whether I wanted to or not. I was to hang in there when it got tough because what did it matter if my plans were usurped by the family's needs?

How, I wondered, could I reconcile that philosophy of

life with what I was doing now — walking out on my noisy household? As I walked and pondered, another Scripture verse came to mind, one from Ecclesiastes where we are reminded there is a time to work and a time to rest. (See Ecclesiastes 3:1-8.) Did that mean a time to hang in there and a time to get away from it all?

I wondered if this meant that the call to lay down our lives didn't mean that we were to be constantly giving without ever taking. Few of us would fast until we were too ill to move. Could it mean that neither should we "lose our lives" until we are too weary to go on? Was the message from Ecclesiastes saying we need to give ourselves to others, and we need to remove ourselves from others, too?

Could it be that walking out on that houseful of children was the most loving and sanity-saving way to deal with the stress of the moment? It *was* giving me perspective. *They're just youngsters, let them make a mess,* I told myself. *It'll get cleaned up tomorrow.*

When I came home I told them they were lovely people and I hoped they would have a good night's sleep. Despite wet bathing suits, scattered popcorn, and wall-to-wall sleeping bags, I decided *I* would have a good night's sleep, too. I went upstairs, certain that for me on that particular night it was better to walk out and come back pleasant than to stick around and be irritable.

As the days went on, the ideas that had come to me on that walk kept returning, as I tried to further sort out the tension between taking care of myself and taking care of others. I saw an analogy between this dilemma and the way we rear our children. For example, let's say you have a six-year-old daughter who is beginning to have some strong ideas of how she wants her life to go. She wants to stay home from school, eat candy bars for breakfast, and stay up until midnight watching adult TV programs. (''All the other kids are doing it.'')

You, her wise mother, say no. ''Honey, you need to go to school, you need to eat a good breakfast, you need to get enough sleep. I don't care what the other kids are doing; adult TV programs will make demands on your thinking that you are not ready to cope with yet.''

So you fix her breakfast, take her to school, tuck her into bed at 8:30 and listen to her prayers. You are not being unreasonable; you want her to be all that God wants her to be, and you work to see that she is not emotionally or physically handicapped in any way that you can control. You know that if you let her have her own way both of you will eventually regret it; you, as she becomes harder and harder to manage, and she, as she finds living her own way harder and harder to deal with.

You and I, as adult women, are composites of both a wise mother and a demanding child. Too often it's the demanding child who gets the upper hand. The reason we don't realize it is that the things we want to do, the things that may be wrong for us, we perceive as good things.

We begin with wise-mother activities — praying, taking care of our households, perhaps earning a living, spending time nurturing our families. Then the wise mother gives way to the demanding child as the activities, the good causes, the social demands, those things that we feel we must do because all the other Christians are doing them, begin to control our lives.

Pretty soon we've lost control. We're out of energy, we're irritable, and we're resentful of one more demand. Yet we know that Christians are not supposed to count the cost. What is happening is that the demanding person in each of us, in order to be like all the other Christians or to do what she perceives a Christian should do, is pushing us far beyond our emotional and physical endurance. It's time for the wise mother to step in and firmly take charge. "Honey," she says to her other self, "you need to get off the merry-go-round. You need proper nourishment and sleep. You need to quit doing so much and rest your body and give yourself some recreation and diversion."

This wise mother is not being selfish or unchristian; she wants her whole person to be all that God wants her to be. She wants her whole self to be emotionally and physically well and in control.

How about your life? What is the wise mother inside of you saying? Is it really all right or even good to walk out on a noisy household for a while? Is it really all right to stop doing and going in order to give yourself a rest and some diversion? What about Jane in the last chapter — what would you like to say to her?

Maybe you're asking if there's a point at which we can go too far and become totally selfish and insensitive to the needs of others; if there is a time when our walking out or taking care of ourselves first is *not* a good thing. Of course there is. But for today our lesson is for the overworked and over-tired woman who has over-planned and over-given. She needs to *quit* being Superlady and find the energy and the balance she needs for every day of her life.

Will you listen to the wise mother inside of you? The

one who says, ''Come, I'll take care of you. There'll be vitamins and nourishment, daily walks and less coffee. There'll be fun and rest and prayers and diversion.'' She has your best interest at heart. She wants to turn that demanding person who does too much into a balanced person God can use in a very special way.

Start With a Doctor

We all hate to visit a doctor when it's not an emergency. Unless we or our children are bleeding or crying in pain we often really don't think it's necessary. Because you probably need a Pap smear and a breast exam anyway (and even if you don't), go ahead and make an appointment.

Tell your primary health care physician what kind of pain or trouble you've been experiencing. Say where it's located and how long it's been going on. If your head or heart or any other part of your body feels strange, say how long it has felt that way. Mention if you are weak or dizzy or extremely irritable. If you feel exhausted, be sure to emphasize this, because almost everyone says they're tired. Mention change in bowel habits or urine output or bladder control. Tell about the stressful situations in your life. Inform the doctor of what medicines you take and how much caffeine and alcohol your body receives daily. If your sleep is disturbed, mention that. Something small to you may be significant to your specific health picture.

Finally, accept the advice offered to you. Trust that your primary health care physician is really concerned about you. If you feel he or she is *not* really concerned about you, it may be time to find a new doctor.

You and the Basic Four

One of the most rewarding things you can do for yourself is to feed yourself properly. If you're feeling really tired, I beg you not to worry about your weight for now. I'm deeply concerned that you get back your energy and that you start feeling like a real person again. For the next few weeks or months let's not be concerned that your figure isn't perfect.

We busy women often make one of two mistakes: we don't eat enough or we eat the wrong foods. Sometimes life gets so busy or so complicated that it's easy to eat the first thing that comes along. Unfortunately the wrong foods work *against* having enough energy instead of *for* it. If you put cheap fuel into your car's gas tank it'll make the engine sluggish after a while. If you don't replenish the fuel, you'll run out of gas. So it is with eating. It's important that you maintain a healthy, balanced diet.

I'd been talking to a group of women about eating correctly and afterward the president, a gracious, professional woman, caught me by the sleeve. "What did you say those four food groups were again?"

I told her and she replied, "You know, it occurred to me as you were talking that I've been eating desserts all day, and I was wondering why I felt so awful! I didn't even realize there *were* four food groups!"

If you are not acquainted with the four food groups, here they are with some examples. Be the wise mother to yourself, choosing your meals from the Basic Four. (*Don't forget breakfast!* It's been said that we age the most from the time we get up until we have our first meal.)

Breakfast

Grains Whole wheat toast or a bowl of oatmeal
Fruits and vegetables Orange juice or cantaloupe, or raisins in your oatmeal
Meat, eggs Two eggs scrambled in 1/2 tsp. butter; bacon or sausage (These are a good source of energy but are high in cholesterol if that is a problem.)
Dairy products A glass of skim milk

Lunch

Grains Whole wheat or seven-grain bread or RyKrisp
Fruits and vegetables Tomato and a banana or carrot and an apple
Meat, poultry, eggs, legumes, and fish Lean sandwich meat or split pea soup (Legumes are a good source of protein when eaten with whole wheat or dairy products.)
Dairy products Cottage cheese (Make a salad with your fruit and vegetable.)

Dinner

Grains Brown rice or whole wheat bread
Fruits and vegetables A green salad and a potato and a peach, pear, or slice of melon
Meat, poultry, eggs, legumes, and fish Chicken, fish, or broiled meat (three ounces is enough) or peanuts or cashews
Dairy products Ice milk

Snacks

Nacho chips, cheese, crackers, skim milk, raw vegetables, soup, grapes, etc.

Oh, yes; drink plenty of *water*. It helps keep your digestive system clean and working well.

Vitamins

A balanced diet in today's world of processed food still doesn't provide all the nutrition we need. Generally accepted is the research of Dr. Terence W. Anderson of the University of British Columbia. He recommends 100 or 150 milligrams of vitamin C on a normal day and 500 milligrams during the first days of a cold or when under stress. (Information from Keith W. Sehnert, MD, *Stress-Unstress*, Minneapolis, MN: Augsburg Publishing House, 1981.) Your health food store and supermarket carry vitamin supplements and specially labeled stress formulas higher in B vitamins and vitamin C for people under stress.

Caffeine and Sugar

A cup of coffee or a Coke gives a great lift to our bodies. They're stimulants. The caffeine in them steps up our bodies and makes us feel good. Then when it wears off, we plummet, and we feel like we desperately need another cup of coffee or another Coke. (In a way we do, to feel "up" again.)

A cup of coffee or two (after a while it takes more than one cup to feel the effects) in the morning, at mid-morning, at lunch, in the afternoon, and again in the evening means your body's system has gone up and down five or more times. Each swing up and down saps your energy. What's making you feel so good for a while is really making you all the more tired.

If you cut your caffeine in half you'll feel a whole lot better. Or better yet, how about dropping it altogether?

Sugar does the same thing to our bodies. Those who've studied the effects of sugar say it also makes many people depressed or anxious.

One summer Bill and I made a quick trip to the wilderness cabin our son John was building for us — a one-room log cabin without electricity or plumbing. There by the door was a glaring, red STOP WORK sign pounded into the door frame by a county inspector. It said we were in violation of the building code and in danger of receiving a penalty. The building could not be occupied. "I wonder what we've done wrong?" Bill asked.

"I don't know, but it can't be too serious. Let's just trust the Lord with the building of our little cabin."

Bill agreed and said he'd call in the morning to see what the violation was all about. We shared our picnic dinner peacefully, looking out over the water. For dessert we ate dark chocolate squares filled with raspberries and cream, a special treat from Canada.

All of a sudden we began to grow anxious over the stop work notice. "Bill, I'm worried. What if this means we can't use the cabin for the rest of the summer?"

Bill was equally concerned. "I hope it's nothing to do with the stove."

"Maybe it's the foundation."

"Maybe it's the porch."

"I hope we're not going to have to fight this with a lawyer." Back and forth we went, growing more and more alarmed.

Then, "What's wrong with us? Why are we so upset? We were so trusting before dinner."

All at once we both knew. It was all that sugar for dessert. The anxiety it produced completely overshadowed our trust. It was proof enough for us that the people who tell us that we need to give up sugar are right.

Diversionary Measures

Following that time described in Chapter 1 when I ran out of energy, I spent long hours and days in bed. My daughter, Mary Therese, cleaned the house, drove my car pool, and shopped for groceries while I did nothing at all. Then my friends started coming. Now understand, I love my friends dearly and they love me, but many of them tend to be just like me — always on the go. They came with good intentions and *lots* of advice. "Pat, I see the Lord has put you in bed so you can spend some time with him." "Pat, here's a study series for you to work on so you won't waste your time." "Pat, here's a theological treatise for you to mull over while you just lie there." "Pat, here are some excellent sermons on tape for you to listen to since you're not busy."

I considered them all and then I protested, "I *can't*. I'm too tired. Everything takes so much effort." My friends couldn't understand that I was literally *out* of energy. Even trying to follow a sermon was too taxing.

My sister Wanda (the one who heads my list of godly people) called and I told her how I couldn't seem to concentrate on all these helpful things people were bringing me so that I would put my time to good use. "I have just the thing for you," she said. "They'll be there in a couple of days."

When the box came I couldn't believe its contents. Inside were three dozen novels. Why, I hadn't thought of reading a novel. Except for summer vacation there just hadn't been the time. I'd always loved reading stories but they were a luxury my present lifestyle didn't include.

I looked over the titles. There were mysteries, westerns, Christian romances, biblical and historical novels. I picked up *Lydia* by Lois Henderson. Propping up the pillows behind me I began to read. Caught up in a story, I began to feel better than I'd felt in days. Suddenly it occurred to me with a sort of mischievous mirth. . . . I was going to enjoy ill health! It was exciting that I was actually going to spend time frivolously on myself.

Day by day as I became stronger I began to pray again and read my Bible. But I still spent a good portion of each day with the books Wanda continued to send. I no longer consider this kind of pastime frivolous. I've found how restorative it can be.

Today when I speak to women about stress and creating a new lifestyle, I ask them to put aside an hour a day just for fun, an hour of nonstressful time just for them. After one speaking engagement one woman called and said she had always wanted to join a bowling league but could never find the time. Now she'd *made* the time and joined. Another set aside that hour to pursue a love from her childhood — embroidering. Still another started hand-crafting puppets.

My daughter Anne, a nuclear medicine student, called one day almost in tears. "I don't know what to do! I have so much homework and it's been such a hard day I can't even concentrate."

"Why don't you give your mind a rest? Do something different, maybe read a novel."

"Oh, Mother, I can't read a novel."

"Then how about doing some of your cross stitch?"

"No, there's not time."

"Then *you* think of it, but do something fun — something not related to school or housework or responsibility."

Later she called back. "I took your advice and I feel ten times better."

"Good, what did you do?"

"I sorted out my high school jewelry. I thought for a while of old friends and old times and I'm really revived."

Like Anne, maybe a novel isn't your thing. But something else is. What can *you* do that's the perfect, non-stressful relaxation for you? (**Warning**: TV is *not* relaxing. It cycles tension because it's produced to keep your emotions on edge so that you don't lose interest.) I promise you restored energy if you'll give yourself some time to really relax.

For me, reading became more than just a way to relax. It

became a tool for dissipating tension. One day last summer one of my sons was missing. I'd gone to pick him up after he'd called from driver's ed and he wasn't there. I waited and looked around. I felt puzzled because this boy was Mr. Dependable; I'd never known him to do something as foolish as accept a ride from a friend when he'd already called home. Certainly he wouldn't just wander off.

I went home, looking for him at every intersection. I tried to remember what he was wearing in case I had to call the police. Grey shorts, grey T-shirt, white socks, and the white tennis shoes we'd just bought him the night before.

When I got home he wasn't there. Meanwhile Joe, who was twenty-one, needed a ride to the city. "Joe, where do you suppose he is?" I hated to be driving Joe to the city when I didn't know where his brother was.

"Oh, Mom, don't worry. By now he's probably been kidnapped and is on his way to New York where he'll be forced into a life of crime, sex, and money-lending."

"Joe, you aren't funny. That's exactly what I was thinking."

On the way back from taking Joe I stopped at the school. He wasn't there. I called home. He wasn't there. I went back to the school but to no avail. I came home and called his friends' houses.

Then the phone rang. "I've been waiting for you, Mom. Where have you been?"

"Where are *you*?" I knew I was going to cry.

"At Mary Therese's. Didn't I tell you on the phone I was here?"

"No."

His sister's house. I should have thought of it. Then I knew I was going to be angry. I cried and was angry at the same time. I hate half crying and half being angry. It sounds like whining.

By the time I was back home with him I felt absolutely awful. I was so disappointed in myself. Why had I cried? Why had I been angry? Why had I worried? What kind of a person was I anyway? Why hadn't I trusted God in the beginning? What a failure!

Wait a minute, I told myself. *You're not a failure. You've been in a stressful situation. This is body-system letdown you're feeling. Now put yourself in a nonstressful situation so you can recuperate.* I took a bunch of grapes from the refrigerator and told the family I was going to take a bath (yes, at 3:30 in the afternoon). On the way upstairs I grabbed the new *Reader's Digest* off the table.

In the tub, I ate the grapes and read all the anecdotes and jokes in the entire issue. (The rest of the month I regretted such extravagance. I usually make the jokes and anecdotes last for at least three weeks!) I laughed quite a bit and before long I felt perfectly fine again.

Many times since, I've used this kind of getaway to help me in difficult times. I remember a time when I felt wounded by the hard words of a friend. As soon as I hung up the phone I knew what I needed to do. I went upstairs and turned on the bath, this time taking my Bible. There, soaking in the warm tub, I asked the Lord's help. A specific Psalm came to mind. Turning the pages carefully so all the markers wouldn't fall into the water, I began to read with a feeling of great expectation. The words were exactly right. "Thank you, Lord, for the healing balm of your Word. And thank you for showing me such a good way to deal with the stress."

Relax, Relax

Have you ever watched a cat prepare for its afternoon nap in the sun? First it stretches every muscle and then curls into a ball and purrs. Want to try it?

Sit on the floor and start *stretching,* arms out, fingers wriggling, neck turning back and forth. Stretch your chest and abdomen. Now lie down and stretch your feet and ankles and legs and pelvis. Feels good, doesn't it? Want to try it again?

Now *relax* your body. Close your eyes and start by thinking of only your right toes. Relax them. Now slowly think about relaxing your right foot, your right ankle, your right leg. Take your time. Now think about relaxing your left toes, your left foot, your left ankle and leg.

Relax your pelvis. Now concentrate on your torso. Think about your right fingers and hand and arm and shoulder. Next do the left side. Think about relaxing your chin and neck and head. Don't hurry. Think about your mouth. Make it smile.

Now how do you feel? All loosened up and peaceful? Will you stretch and relax your physical body every day?

Now comes the part where you'll want to purr. It's my favorite. It takes two people for this one but it's easy to get someone to help you if you promise to do the same for your partner. (This is a wonderful thing for a wife and husband to do.) You can even go first and show how it's done.

Let the other person lie on the floor with their foot in your lap. Now pour a little oil or lotion on the foot and softly rub it in. Gently massage and rotate each toe and then give each toe a little tug. Rub your thumb up and down the bottom of the foot several times beginning at the heel and working up toward the toes.

Massage the ball of the foot, then the top. Hold the foot gently and rotate its ankle. End with a little tug on the leg. Now do the other foot. But make sure your partner doesn't go to sleep right there on the floor before you get your turn!

There's one more gift you can give to your body — adequate sleep. At night, go to bed. Turn off the TV without watching the news. Read a Psalm or listen to a tape of Scripture after you're in bed. Promise yourself you'll get seven to eight hours of sleep every night.

During the day, take a nap. Put your head on your desk or on the kitchen table at home. Pray the Lord's Prayer slowly twice. Even if you sleep only ten or twenty minutes you'll feel like a whole new you.

The bunker where Winston Churchill took his famous daily naps can still be visited. He claimed that a good nap could make one day into two.

Listen to these interesting words from Judson Cornwall:

> Directed inactivity is as spiritual as directed activity, and all who will bear His yoke must learn this. Sometimes the most spiritual thing a person can do is sleep or enjoy recreation or just take time to be with

the family. When this is done under divine direction, it will not cost heaven's kingdom any service, and it will enable us to be more productive servants when it is time to get back into the harness again. . . . As surely as the music score, the rest is to be observed equally with the notes. (Judson Cornwall, *Let Us Abide,* South Plainfield, NJ: Bridge Pub. Co., 1977.)

Take a Hike

Every book I've ever read on handling stress endorses (no, *commands*) a daily twenty-minute walk — not in a cozy, covered shopping mall, but outdoors. At first I rejected this advice, but my doctor insisted. He made walking outdoors for twenty minutes each day an absolute must. So I went, but only because I felt I had to.

Believe me, nothing special happened between me and the outdoors on that first walk — or on the second or third. It was like being with a casual acquaintance with whom I was reluctant to get involved, like being forced into seeing this person every day, but he just didn't do anything for me.

But I kept at it to please the doctor. Besides, it *was* autumn, and the leaves did crackle underfoot. The air *was* crispy, not unlike that first bite of a delicious apple in October. Once I'd jostled myself away from the house the walking didn't seem too bad.

Then it rained. Rain that flattened my hair and slid unwelcome down my collar. Chilling rain that raised goose bumps on my arms beneath my raincoat. Rain then turned the sky and earth into one grey, water-soaked abyss. The experts said twenty minutes a day. Doggedly I walked. Just sticking with it made it something of a triumph.

When it got cold I pulled on lined boots, zipped up my down coat, and kept my hands in my pockets. On the trail, blackberry vines curled listlessly and summer's stately maples looked ashamed of their nakedness. Yet the cold air was a challenge, a competitor. I'd show it! I'd stay longer than twenty minutes.

I found that some days the whole sky above me was a deep and comforting shade of blue. I didn't remember ever really noticing when the yellow-green leaves of spring peered from their winter-blackened branches. By the middle of March I carried my down coat home in my arms and let the wind blow the curl from my hair. I wondered what it was that smelled so good.

Then summer came. I often walked just before twilight, because that's when the breeze and setting sun choreographed the evening's light show. Shimmering leaves tap danced in place; waves flash danced in glittering rows; orchid clouds pirouetted across the horizon. I found I was going eagerly each night, not wanting to miss the entertainment.

When the cycle was complete and autumn had returned, so had my energy. I didn't have a doctor standing over me, the stress books were gathering dust on my office shelf, yet I walked. I went because my reluctant friendship had blossomed into an affair. I found I was in love with walking outdoors. We were more than friends. Walking through a park or down a country road or along the beach was something akin to eyes meeting across the room. There was an electricity — that special something only lovers share.

Now there comes a time each day when I turn off the screen on my word processor, reach for a sweater, a raincoat, or a parka, and hurry out to keep my daily tryst. *How can it be,* I ask as I walk, *that only a little over a year ago we didn't even know each other?*

The High Cost of Recovery

As I'm sure you have realized by now, it's going to take some time to properly care for yourself. There's extra food to prepare and more time spent eating it. Reading or doing something fun each day takes a big commitment. Stretching, relaxing, massaging, and getting enough sleep are well worth the trouble, but they also take time. Then there's that all-important commitment to the twenty-minute walk.

That's just what taking care of yourself needs to be — a commitment to your good health, to your restored energy, to *you* feeling good again.

Where is the time going to come from?

Turn the page. I have a suggestion I think you're going to like.

EIGHT
Sixteen Ways to Say No

"Is there someone here who will volunteer?" I asked at a workshop. A young woman raised her hand and came to the microphone. While she was approaching, I spoke to the audience. "Saying no is one of the hardest tasks we women have to do in order to have enough energy. In fact, it's so hard we're going to practice it this afternoon."

I turned to the volunteer whose name was Patti. "Now pretend you're overburdened with work. You're weary to your toes and you feel cross and irritable. You know you can't take on another responsibility so whatever I ask you to do, you're going to answer no."

Pretending to call her on the phone I introduced myself and asked her if she would take a foreign student into her home for the summer.

"No, I can't."

"But if you don't take him thirty-five other students can't come."

"No."

"I hear you're a Christian. This student is a Hindu and you can evangelize him if he's in your home."

"N . . . no."

"This is a chance to spread the gospel."

She wavered. The audience could tell she was tempted. "I'll have to ask my husband."

"Please. . . . "

"Oh, I'll do it," she exploded.

The audience burst into laughter. We could all see ourselves. Even though Patti knew she couldn't bear the load of one more thing she'd gone ahead and agreed to it. Most of us react the same way when our guilt strings are pulled hard enough.

We later ended the workshop in one-to-one prayer. Patti, the volunteer, wept over the burden she carried daily. She had so much responsibility weighing her down that it was crushing her. She said her tears were partly because she had come to see that much of this burden was her own fault. She was carrying responsibility that belonged to others and then she was resenting them because she had so much to do.

Why Is Saying No So Hard?

Why did Patti find it so hard to say no? Because, like us, she feels she has to say yes when there is a need. If someone has a need we feel we have to help that person. Yet too often our response is not rooted in what Jesus would have us do, but rather in the way we think we must perform.

From the time my friend Jon was twelve years old he had said he wanted to be a priest. His mother was so proud of him. Often he was excused from work around the house because "Jon has to study." He was given extra gifts and consideration because "Jon's our special one." It was unthinkable that Jon would pursue any other career.

At college he met and fell in love with Marcy — pretty, carefree Marcy. They spent long hours talking, and during one of those talks Jon came to realize that he really didn't want to be a priest. Today, years later, he's a fine teacher. Unfortunately, that's not the end of the story.

Inside of Jon's mind is a tape recording that plays over and over, "Jon's special. He's going to be a priest." But sometimes he hears it this way, "Jon's not special now. He's not a priest." Jon doesn't know it's only an old tape that's playing. He's heard it so often, it's a part of his life. Consequently he finds he must make up for his career decision. He works harder than any other teacher at school. At church, no matter what he's asked to do, he does it. He and Marcy have two children who take second place to the work that must be done elsewhere. Once someone pointed out to him that he didn't need to teach a Bible study, that there was one over on the next street. That advice made him angry. Jon *needed* to teach it; it helped him feel good about himself.

Marcy knew that if she had done things differently, Jon would be a priest today. So she began to believe the not-so-subtle words of her mother-in-law — that she'd taken a good man from the Lord's full-time work. Although Marcy hates Jon's overinvolvement, she encourages him, often joins him. It makes up for what she's done.

One day in a long, painful session she told how much she wanted to be just an ordinary person, living an ordinary Christian life with an ordinary husband. But as long as Jon keeps struggling to make up for "not being special" she knows he'll always be committed first to some kind of cause — at least as long as his mother is still alive.

Too often we become overburdened because we don't take time to distinguish between our wills and the Lord's will. Zoanne Wilkie tells this story about herself:

> Sometimes my mercy runs amuck. Once I met a young woman in dire straits and invited her home to live with us. I wanted to cure all the unhappiness in her life and make her life wonderful.
>
> Before too long, life at our house was awful for everyone as this woman became more and more demanding. I woke up every morning dreading the day.
>
> Finally I went to the Lord and said, "Father, can I let her go?"
>
> His answer totally surprised me. "I never wanted you to take her in the first place."
>
> I learned that when we do great and generous acts for other people it has to be because the Lord has led us, not because we want to make them or ourselves wonderful.

To Colleen, another friend, saying no was unthinkable. Her marriage was far from rewarding. Her son kept failing at school. Life had been filled with other disappointments as well. Then she found the world of volunteer work, a world that applauded superhuman efforts on its behalf. The more she worked at community causes, the more people appreciated her and the better she felt. Colleen, now bone-weary all of the time, can't stop. She sees herself as a successful person only as long as she doesn't say no.

Ultimately, this is what is so hard about saying no to others. Our self-image, the way we see ourselves, is tied to our performance. If we perform well we think we must be OK. Even as little girls our mothers made this clear. ("You've tied your own shoes, what a good girl!") If we don't perform well — according to the world's standards — then we think we've failed. For so many of us it's hard to say no and feel good about ourselves at the same time.

Jesus, so filled with compassion for those he lived among, had to say no. He had to go away to pray. He had to spend time alone with his disciples so they could be taught. It's curious that Jesus, who left so many people unhealed and untaught, could say at the end of his life, "Father . . . I glorified you on earth by accomplishing the work that you gave me to do" (John 17:1,4). This example tells us what we need to heed: It's not up to us to do it all.

Author and Bible teacher Denise Adler says this:

> I would say to the Christian woman . . . that she should take a good hard look at her activities and see where she has taken on a responsibility that isn't for her. It could even be that a perfect job for her situation and talent is going undone while she strug-

gles at something that isn't what the Holy Spirit intended for her. In addition, when any of us undertakes a work that is not meant for us, we deprive the person for whom it was meant in the first place.

Saying No to Those We Love

Sometimes it's the people who love us the most who make it the most difficult to say no even when we know we should. Our family managed to obtain four tickets for the track and field events of the Olympic Games held in Los Angeles. That meant that Bill and our boys, ages eleven, fifteen, and twenty-one, looked forward all winter to the big event. It was assumed I'd go along for the ride even though I didn't have a ticket.

However, the more I listened to the plans and heard about driving twelve hours at a time, sleeping in the car, and getting up early to watch the marathoners, the more I began to understand the stamina this trip was going to require — stamina I knew I didn't have.

Then one day I realized I didn't have to go, that I shouldn't go, that, in fact, my body was telling me *not* to go. Certainly four capable people could manage their meals and laundry without me. I prayed about it and felt at peace with my decision, even though it was the first vacation I would ever miss.

The first one to react was my mother. She had been looking forward to me seeing my brother Ralph who lived in southern California. "But Ralph will be so disappointed if you don't come."

"I know, Mom, but the ride seems too much for me right now."

"You should be with your family."

"They can manage without me."

"Your poor brother. What's he going to think?"

Finding that out didn't take too long because Ralph called me the next week. "I hear you're not coming."

"It's too far."

"Donna and I have been looking forward to seeing you."

"I just don't feel I have the energy to make the trip."

"We've got a king-size bed all ready for you and Bill. We'll take you out to dinner. We'll have a good time."

"I don't know, Ralph. I'll think about it."

At home the pressure was more subtle. Since I'd always gone on vacation this was a change that Bill wasn't ready for. He understood my need to stay home and rest but he wanted me to go, too. As a result, he gave me two messages, affirming and nonaffirming. First he said, "I understand your need to stay home, but I'm really going to miss you." Then he said, "You've made a wise choice, but it's not too late to change your mind. Why don't you think it over some more?"

"No, I really don't want to go."

So at last it was settled. I'd said no. Except it wasn't settled. It's hard for people to hear what you're saying when they don't want to hear it.

My mother, brother, and particularly Bill all loved me so much they just couldn't believe that my idea of what was good for me was better than their idea of what was good. The pressure continuing from Bill was done with love. "Are you sure you don't want to go?"

"I'm sure."

"I'll miss you."

"I'll miss you, too."

"I can't believe I'm going without you."

"I can't believe it, either."

"If you want to come you can always change your mind at the last minute."

"I want to stay home."

With a sad look, "I'm already lonely."

No answer from me. What could I say?

The day they left, Joe found that he could possibly get an extra ticket for two days of the games. Bill began to plan how I could fly down and join them. I was frying chicken for them to take for their dinner and weeping into the batter. *Isn't anyone listening to me? I've said no so many times in so many ways!*

Finally I felt so selfish I couldn't stand it. "Dear God, I'm so sure I should stay home, but if the tickets are available I'll go." I turned to Bill. "If you can pick up the tickets I'll fly down."

He was delighted.

The next morning in my prayer time I understood that this wasn't a test of my willingness to lay down my life: You can hardly raise a family and not learn that lesson. But it was a test of whether I would do what I knew I should do or if I would do what someone else wanted me to do.

A little later Bill called from San Francisco where

they'd driven 810 miles without stopping. "We're having a wonderful time but I feel like half of me is missing. I'll call you as soon as we hear about the tickets."

"I really don't want to come."

"Let's see if we can get the tickets and then we'll decide."

I hung up and my head started aching, a sign of too much stress. I thought, *How do I deal with this situation through which I'm trying to regain my energy at such cost?* "Dear God, please help me."

Bill called that evening. "San Francisco is wonderful! We walked all the places you and I walked last September and I remembered how much fun we had. (Pause) Then I remembered that it wasn't fun for you, you were so tired. (Pause) We're able to get the extra tickets but I don't think you should come. Why don't you stay home and rest?"

"Thank you, Bill. Thank you for not pushing me anymore."

When I hung up I thanked the Lord with all my heart. Then I went for a walk. By the time I got back the headache was gone and I was beginning to feel good. I'd said no when I knew I should, and Bill, the one who loves me the most, had finally heard.

How to Say No

If saying no is as hard for you as it is for most people, here are a few ways to say no that might help you in the future.

Perfectly valid NO

"I've been out three nights this week. I'm staying home and watching TV with the kids." Say it like you mean it.

Let's-share-the-responsibility NO

"I'm certain you can find someone else who will enjoy cleaning up after the meeting as much as I used to."

Singing NO

This will help you keep it light and yet not give in. Use it on the teenage daughter who's pushing you to take her baby-sitting job because her plans have changed. Sing the scale up and down, using the word *no, no, no,* instead of *do, re, mi*. Smile while singing.

Let-someone-else-say-no-for-you NO

(It's weak, perhaps, but in one of those desperate situation-desperate measure times it's OK to be weak.) "Honey, will you run next door and tell nice Mrs. Jones that I can't come to her home party this week?"

No-after-saying-yes NO

"I've made a mistake. I shouldn't have committed myself. I'm sorry, I'll have to back out." Hang up the phone and give a huge sigh of relief.

Five-star NO

(There's no comeback for this.) "I'll have to pass it up."

Not-right-now NO

"I've done it before and I'll do it in the future, but I can't do it now."

Get-tough NO

(This usually comes at the end of a parent/teenage wrangle when the teenager wants to throw an unchaperoned party.) "I'm the mother. You're the kid. The answer's no."

I-wish-I-could NO

"I'd love to do this. I know it's going to be interesting. I've always wanted to do it, but I'm totally unable to do it now."

Pass-the-buck NO

"I'm busy that day, but I know Virginia would love to do it. (Please don't mention I suggested her name.)"

Polite NO

"I'm sorry, but my schedule doesn't permit me to take on any more obligations this (pick one) week/month/year/decade."

No-way NO

This one is for a teenage son who wants you to call your friends for a ride so he can have the car. Look directly in his eyes, smile, enunciate clearly. Say no.

Diplomatic NO

"It was so kind of you to think of me. I'm flattered you asked. I'm sorry I won't be able to do it."

Cowardly NO

Backed into a corner? Feeling low on energy or courage or both? Feeling somewhat desperate? Use this one: "My husband/mother/child doesn't want me to do that."

Body-language NO

(This is for people who don't go home even when you've said how tired you are.) Stand up. Stretch. Frown a little. Leave room. Don't come back.

Absolute NO

"I cannot do this. I don't have the desire, the time, the interest, or the energy. No. Absolutely not. Never." (Save this one for special occasions.)

NINE

The Ultimate in Energy: Getting to Know Christ

It was April, over six months since I'd run out of energy. I was feeling pretty much like myself, yet I wasn't completely fine, either. *What's taking so long?* I asked myself many times.

I sat in the sunshine on the deck with another new book from Wanda, this one not a novel. In it the author talked about how the hurts of the past affect our present responses. She gave numerous examples of people helped to wholeness when they, through the Holy Spirit, remembered old hurts and asked Jesus to walk with them through the past and heal them.

As I read, I sensed something special was going to happen. *Lord, how does this book apply to me?* Then it came to my mind that part of the weariness in my body was related to our son, Paul.

Paul had been shot by accident. When we arrived at the hospital we were told that his neurological activity was about five percent. That meant that his brain was nearly gone. Right then we asked God for a miracle. We believed that God, who had raised up Lazarus, dead for four days, could raise up Paul — that to God nothing was impossible. When morning came, Paul died.

All during the funeral and the long days that followed all we could do was try to believe that God's ways are higher than our ways. Our pain was intense.

Then, one and a half years later, Bill's heart failed. (This was not surprising, since major illness often follows the death of a beloved person.) There in the hospital with Bill looking so much like Paul and not getting any better, and Paul having died, something inside of me came to believe that the reason we lost Paul was that I hadn't had enough faith. If only I'd believed more, Paul would have lived. Therefore, I worried that I didn't have enough faith for God to heal Bill, either, and Bill would die, too. That was when the strange feelings had first come; that was when the peculiar weariness that had plagued me all summer had begun; that was when the lack of energy I'd felt at the retreat had originated. Even though Bill had not died, here was the root reason that I still didn't have all my energy back.

There on the deck as I thought of all this, I knew it was too big for me to handle alone. I thought of a friend who is experienced in praying for the healing of emotions. I went right to her house and poured it all out.

"Oh, Joyce, I've been thinking all this time that if only I'd had more faith Paul wouldn't have died."

She wrapped loving arms around me and I rested my head on her broad shoulder. "Let's go back to the hospital," she said. "Picture yourself there and picture Paul hooked up to the machines and lying so still. Now look for Jesus. Do you see him?"

I said I could.

"Now tell Jesus all about it. Tell him how you feel."

In my mental picture I couldn't talk. I could only look at Jesus. Then he took me in his comforting arms. I knew then that all the sorrow I'd felt at losing Paul he'd suffered with me.

As Joyce prayed I came to realize that my faith had never been on the line in deciding whether Paul would receive a miracle healing or not.

When Joyce finished praying, I sighed an enormous sigh and felt like ten tons had dropped from me. I wiped away my tears. It felt so good to let Christ heal all the places that had hurt for so long. Later when I charted the restoration of my energy, that day stood as a major milestone.

Jesus himself said, "Come to me, all you who labor and are burdened, and I will give you rest" (Matthew 11:28). Looking to Christ's peace, asking him to see beneath the surface of my feelings, and then praying with a friend had brought the healing I needed.

Making contact with Christ is something that can happen in many ways. In this chapter we are going to look at some of the ways we can come to him and find the rest that he has promised.

Getting Under the Surface

I was sitting in a restaurant near the airport with a friend who had just come into town. As we talked I felt my back and shoulders tense with pain. Recognizing the pain as a stress symptom, I asked the Lord, "What's going on here?'' Then I waited for an answer. Understanding came to my mind. Years ago this friend often had been critical to the extreme. Without consciously knowing it, I was steeling myself for his criticism.

As soon as I realized what I was doing, I relaxed. He had changed and so had I. Even if he was critical it wouldn't be that big of a deal today. From then on I could enjoy the rest of our conversation.

There are so many ways, so many times, when we can listen to what our bodies are saying to us about our under-the-surface feelings. What does this backache really mean? What is this headache really saying? Ask the Holy Spirit to let you know. Sometimes it's healing enough just to know what's causing the physical symptom.

Maybe it's something you need to talk over with a friend. We do need each other. Is there one person you can think of who will truly listen to you over and over for as long as it takes? This kind of friend doesn't come along all that often, but when she does, she's priceless. If you have such a person, just talking out your worries should throw a lot of light on what's bothering you.

Possibly it's time for a professional counselor. When you go for that medical appointment, tell your primary health care physician that you want to get to the bottom of some things and ask for suggestions of where to go for help.

Maybe for now you want to go it on your own. I was touched by something that a woman wrote about herself in a book I read. The author had been depressed for over five years. Her life had become a dull, dreary, monotonous grey. Then she began to write daily letters to her doctor, telling him about her day or her dreams for her life or her observations of God's beautiful earth. She wrote to her doctor twice a day for over six months and remarkable things began to happen. She said that the writing straightened out the whole world for her. Not only that, but her writing was the beginning of her first best-selling novel.

Today we have a name for what this woman did: It's called *journaling*. Instead of writing to a doctor, many people record their daily lives and thoughts in a notebook. For myself, I keep a journal in which everything is written to Christ.

If this is something that appeals to you, begin by buying a large spiral notebook and designate it for *you*, not the family. Every day write in it whatever it is *you* want to write. Penmanship, spelling, and grammar are not important. You won't need a dictionary or a thesaurus. No one is ever going to read this but you and the Lord.

Sometimes you may want to make it a letter to him. Sometimes you'll just want to record what's been going on in the family and how you feel about it. Sometimes you may want to write about what a friend said that touched you, or something that hurt you or made you angry. When there is no one you can really talk to, writing down your thoughts helps a great deal. Many times I've come to a solution just by writing down a problem. It's a good place to record accomplishments and disappointments, especially the little things that don't seem to matter to anyone but you. Who knows, the writing that forms the basis of your prayer today may be the same writing that forms the basis of your novel tomorrow!

Our Personal Volcano

In the first part of this book we took a good, hard look at stress symptoms. Let's consider the possibility that many times these symptoms are the rocky top layer of a volcanic mountain. The sharp layer underneath the top layer is guilt and anger, while the next layer is the pebbly grey area of hurts. The fourth layer is the sand of misunderstanding and feeling unneeded. (These hurts are types of non-reciprocity.) The bottom layer is our ego. It's so fragile that too much pressure from the layers above can cause it to explode and spew its volcanic ash far and wide. One of the ways to get the pressure off that bottom layer is to drill from the top.

A man who was both friend and relative came to visit one day and I invited him to come with me on my walk. There were such deep furrows of concern on his face I thought maybe a walk would help.

By the time we came to the corner he was telling me that the doctor had called the spots in front of his eyes stress symptoms. Because our friendship was one of long standing I felt it would be all right to inquire as to whether these symptoms were the top layer of Rob's personal volcano. "Rob, do you think you could be feeling guilty about something or angry at someone?"

"No!" He was emphatic. A car whipped past us and made us both shiver in its wind. For a while we walked in silence. Finally he said, "OK, I guess I am."

He told me how angry he was at his daughter because she'd dropped out of school and was bumming around instead of working. Then he added that if he'd been a better father to her he knew she would have stayed in school.

"You're really hurt, aren't you?"

A few winter birds chattered in the cold. Rob pulled his coat tighter. Finally he admitted, "Yes, I am." He began to really talk. He'd done so much for his daughter. He'd given so much, helped out so often, tried to meet her needs, made such sacrifices, and she didn't appreciate any of it. What's more, she didn't need him at all now that she had this stupid boyfriend.

As in all of us at one time or another, in Rob's personal volcano, the lava was bubbling. Then came the hard part for me because I didn't know how he was going to take what I wanted to say next. "Will you ask God to forgive you for your anger at your daughter, and ask God to forgive you for the times you feel you weren't a good father?"

I was glad we were walking because it helped pass the time in which he didn't say anything at all. Then I heard, "OK."

"Now will you forgive your daughter?"

"I can't." More walking. More silence. "OK, I will."

"Rob, I know someone who appreciates you, understands you, and needs you."

He looked at me suspiciously, saying, "Who?"

"Jesus." We'd taken a detour and were tramping through some underbrush along the side of a ravine. At the bottom we came to a lake with the sun sparkling on its icy waters.

Rob didn't tell me what had gone on in his mind or his soul as we made our way down to the beach but when I looked at him I saw his face was as free of furrows as I'd seen it in a long time. All he said was, "The spots before my eyes are gone."

A churning volcano had been diffused. Christ's healing forgiveness had found him. In Rob's life, a mountain had been moved.

Whatever way you find to make contact with Christ in this matter of understanding your feelings, whether it's asking the Holy Spirit's help to be healed of the past, or whether it's going to a friend or a professional counselor or keeping a journal or diffusing a volcano with forgiveness, you'll feel the difference in your life. When we begin to sort out our inner feelings it's amazing how much more energy we have.

The Great Thief of Energy

A Scripture passage from the Gospel of Matthew sheds an interesting light on the great thief of energy in Christ's life:

> Then the devil took him up to a very high mountain, and showed him all the kingdoms of the world in their magnificence, and he said to him, "All these I shall give to you, if you will prostrate yourself and worship me." At this, Jesus said to him, "Get away, Satan! It is written: 'The Lord, your God, shall you worship and him alone shall you serve' " (Matthew 4:8-10).

So *that's* how the devil works, by offering us great things if only we will allow him to rob us of all our energy.

One way this happens is when we become too busy to care for our bodies so that we become not only ineffective in our work but weary and grumpy as well.

You get to the point where one more good cause can be the final straw. So can one more doubt, one more worry, and one more crisis. The robbery is so subtle, you don't know your energy is gone until you reach for it and it's not there.

How do you get your energy back? One way, as I already said, is to *take care of your physical body.* That's like keeping the house locked so the thief can't just walk in.

The next way is to *demand* that unhealthy, energy-sapping forces *leave* when you find them on the premises. In a way, you must say, "Get out of here, Satan!" and *mean* it when you say it because you have the power to deal with this enemy. In the story of Christ's temptation, the devil had power, yes; but Jesus was much more powerful because he was able to draw upon the power of the Holy Spirit and that Spirit is in you, too! If this is the way Jesus dealt with the devil, you can do the same.

So first we lock our house against the devil with sensible care. Second, using the powerful name of Jesus, we boot that thief out when we find him present. Third, we put up a barbed-wire fence. We read about this barbed wire in Ephesians 6. It's called the "armor of God," and we're given steps to take to keep ourselves protected.

> Therefore, put on the armor of God, that you may be able to resist on the evil day and, having done everything, to hold your ground. So stand fast with

> your loins girded in truth, clothed with righteousness as a breastplate, and your feet shod in readiness for the gospel of peace. In all circumstances, hold faith as a shield, to quench all [the] flaming arrows of the evil one. And take the helmet of salvation and the sword of the Spirit, which is the word of God (Ephesians 6:13-17).

How does this work to protect us? A story by Midge Candee in *Guideposts* magazine explained it well.

> I was suffering from a deep mental depression, which left me unable to cope with even the simplest household chores. Despite the very best psychiatric treatment, my condition didn't improve. How baffling it was! There was no problem in my marriage — my husband, Mark, was kind, gentle, and supportive — and the doctors could find no imbalance in my body chemistry, or any reason for me to be in such a state of mind. After I'd been hospitalized ten months the doctors told Mark that he should "prepare for the long haul."
>
> While this was going on, Mark was under the additional pressure of starting a new job and making arrangements for our eleven-year-old son, John, to be looked after. I knew how they were suffering, but I just could not be motivated.
>
> All along Mark was praying for a miracle and trusting the Lord for my healing — as were the members of many prayer groups. And just when my prospects seemed worst, two pray-ers at Adriel Retreat in Lake Ariel, Pennsylvania, called Mark with a strange-sounding idea. God had revealed to them,

they said, that Mark should study the "armor of God" section of Ephesians and that he should phone me each morning at the hospital so together we could read these passages and act out the putting on of God's armor.

When Mark brought it up to me I felt it was bizarre — but he persuaded me that we ought at least to try it. So with the telephone receiver propped under my ear, I rather sullenly went through the motions.

On that first day I acted out the verses just to please Mark. But within a few days, something began to happen. The dreadful feeling of uselessness began to disappear. Visualizing and speaking this section of Scripture out loud were causing a change in me. Day after day we continued to put on God's armor and unbelievably, within ten days I was discharged from the hospital, whole and well; no further treatment was required.

I know my physicians were superbly equipped to heal my flesh. But the Word of God, "sharper than any two-edged sword" (Hebrews 4:12), freed me from the oppression of spirit I was under.

To this day, ten years later, Mark and I continue to act out those Ephesians Scriptures when we get up in the morning. For we know that we're always vulnerable to mental stress, discouragement, anxiety, and depression. And we believe that putting on the whole armor of God is the best way to meet the day as confident soldiers.

1. Gird your loins with truth. Admit that God wants you to be positive and optimistic.

2. Strap on the breastplate of righteousness and declare that His love and your faith will stop harmful feelings from entering your heart.

3. Wear the gospel of peace on your feet. Actually bend down and slip on a pair of "shoes." Imagine that you are standing on the Word of God and stepping out into a bright new world of mental well-being.

4. Take up the shield of faith. Say out loud, "Lord, I know you will protect me from evil."

5. Put the helmet of salvation on your head. Thank God in Jesus' name for protecting your mind from depression and stress.

6. Finally grasp the hilt of the sword of the Spirit "which is the Word of God." Raise it high over your head, saying, "Lord, I know this is Your Word and with it I can conquer all my problems" (Midge Candee, "How to Dress for Stress," *Guideposts*, October 1983).

Perhaps you're thinking, "But I've *tried* praying and my life is still a mess. Prayer seems to be a waste if you ask me."

Everyone is different. Christ helped Midge Candee improve her life by placing his words within her so that Christ-inspired positive thinking was enough to restore her energy. Christ may lead another woman to confide in a friend or counselor. For you and others, Christ's healing power may come in the form of learning to help yourself — by taking yourself to the doctor for treatment, by taking better care of your body, or by saying no to those who would sap you of energy. The point is, prayer is never a waste. But when we pray, we can't always just mutter words and then expect Jesus to do the rest of the work. What often happens is that Christ places the seed of an idea in us, and from that seed we grow our own idea for what to do and how then to go do it.

Yes, negativity will try to rob our energy in many ways, but we can lock that devil out, boot him out, and keep him out!

A Surprising Word About Prayer

I still remember how hard it was to pray those first few days and weeks after I ran out of energy. I remember my friends insisting God had allowed this to happen so I could spend more time in prayer. I also still remember, despite my lack of prayer during this time, the presence of God that was with me throughout each day.

What I'm saying here is that during those times when you haven't the energy to pray, then don't pray. If you've been faithful in prayer, then in this season of drought those prayer roots you put down earlier will continue to keep your life fruitful. (See Jeremiah 17:7-8.)

If you've not prayed much before this, don't worry. Pray the "armor" prayer adapted from Ephesians found in the previous section of this book and call it a day. For now, just *wanting* to pray more is prayer enough. It's OK not to be a spiritual giant; it's OK not to be an intercessor for now. But here's the catch: *it is also OK to ask others to pray for you.*

In addition to my family's prayers for me, I asked the same group of friends to pray for me over and over until I was embarrassed to request so much prayer and be so needy. But after I was strong again one of them prayed, "Father, we thank you that you have allowed us to be a part of Pat's recuperation and thank you for showing us what you can do."

Asking others to pray for us blesses them. Especially if you have always been a "tower of strength." It also endears you to them as nothing else can do. (Towers of strength usually are not too endearing.) I believe it also endears us to God when we admit that not only do we need the help of a Higher Power but the help of our brothers and sisters as well.

Usually, getting our energy back after it's run out doesn't happen with just one prayer unless God works a miracle. For most people the energy restoration process is like taking a starving refugee child into your home. You don't pray over her and give her one good meal and expect her malnutrition to be gone and her memories healed. No, it's a process that takes time — repeated prayer and repeated meals. Most often the getting better happens gradually. That's why we need continual prayer.

Eventually your strength will come back and you can begin to pray and intercede again. But when you are needy, let others hold you up in prayer.

God's Word

Reading Scripture doesn't take as much energy as prayer. You can prop yourself up in the bathtub or bed and read the Sermon on the Mount and feel better for having made the effort.

For starters, give yourself a treat of some of the Bible's most beloved passages. The following are short, familiar, comforting passages. As you read each one, let the age-old words seep into your soul and warm your heart.

Day 1: Psalm 23
Day 2: Matthew 6:9-13
Day 3: Matthew 5:2-12
Day 4: Isaiah 43:1-3
Day 5: Philippians 4:4-6
Day 6: John 3:16; 1 John 1:9
Day 7: Psalm 103:1-5

The following week read as the Gospel of John tells of seven different miracles of Jesus. It's fun to watch the progression as each one becomes more dramatic and incredible than the one before, as the Gospel writer proves to readers that Jesus really is the Son of God. Remember, it's all right just to read a little and it's OK not to study for now; it's all right just to be comforted.

Day 1: John 2:1-11
Day 2: John 4:46-53
Day 3: John 5:2-9
Day 4: John 6:1-13
Day 5: John 6:16-21
Day 6: John 9:1-7
Day 7: John 11:32-45

The third week, go for the stories. If Nielsen were to poll Christians on the Bible stories they love the most, I'm sure the following would be at the top of the ratings:

Day 1: Luke 2:1-20
Day 2: Genesis 37:23-36, chapters 39-45
Day 3: Luke 10:29-37
Day 4: 1 Samuel 17:19-50
Day 5: Luke 11:14-23
Day 6: Luke 19:1-10
Day 7: Luke 24:1-9

God's Word brings healing and strength, encouragement and miracles. We who are weary should not miss out on the very help we need the most.

Contact With Christ

It started with a phone call. The hard-to-hear news about someone I loved deeply, coupled with some words I'd overheard a few days before, told me what I didn't want to know.

For a few days after hearing it I thought I was OK, that I was strong enough, that this wasn't going to affect me. I prayed earnestly about the situation and the rest of the time tried not to think about it. Then I began waking in the middle of the night. I had been feeling so good and now during the day I was feeling so tired. In my shoulder was a tight, painful muscle. *These are stress symptoms,* I told myself one morning. I didn't relate them to the hurtful news, but I did make sure to take it easy for the rest of the day.

By the next morning as Bill and I started our morning

prayers I began to see what I'd been hiding from myself. The bad news I thought I was handling was actually tearing me apart. And there was no one I could tell without uncovering someone else's life.

Then as I was sitting there in bed a picture came to my mind. It was of a swaybacked donkey staggering under a heavy load, barely plodding up a steep cobblestone road, while its weariness showed in every footstep.

In the picture, the weary donkey came and stood before Jesus. One by one Jesus removed the burdens from the donkey's back and placed them on his own back. As soon as he placed them on his back they disappeared. He kept unloading the donkey's burdens until it stood empty, free. Along with this picture came the words of Jesus: "Come to me, all you who labor and are burdened, and I will give you rest" (Matthew 11:28).

I knew that I was that donkey and that I was to bring my heavy burden to Jesus. In this picture that was so clear in my mind, I stood before him. "Here, Lord, here is the problem I've carried around for the past few days." He took it. I don't know what he did with it, but it wasn't weighing me down anymore. I tried to analyze it. How had it happened? I felt like the blind man who reported to the Pharisees, "I was blind and now I see." I could say, "I was burdened and now I'm free."

Each of us has had times when we were heavily laden. Our burdens, so uniform in heaviness, were probably diversified in content. Yet to each of us Jesus has sent an invitation: "If you are weary and overburdened and out of energy, come to me."

Some will bring a grudge about a hurt done to them that

was so terrible that they can't forgive it on their own. Some will bring bitterness, a root that has grown for so long and gone so deep that they haven't the energy to pull it up and be rid of it.

Some will bring past sin — adultery, abortion, stealing, a lie that hurt someone else, blasphemy, superstitiousness, prejudice, and others.

Many will bring the burdens of life — rejection, financial problems, disease, pain, broken dreams. Others will bring the burdens of the heart — loved ones who have chosen an alternate lifestyle, loved ones who appear indifferent to all the love poured out on them.

It shouldn't be too hard to see ourselves as the out-of-energy, overburdened donkey weighed down by life's situations. Can we also see ourselves standing before Jesus and letting him unload the wearisome weight we've been carrying for so long? If we can picture that, then it shouldn't be too hard to see that burden disappear, absorbed by Jesus who is so willing to carry our burdens for us.

Try to do it now. Bring to Christ all the troubles we've talked about in this book. Bring him your stress symptoms; bring him your need to take good care of yourself; bring him your struggle with your neediness and those situations which rob your energy.

Bring him *you*. "Here I am, Jesus. I accept the invitation to trust you with this painful situation. I accept the invitation to let you help me sort out my overburdened life. I accept your invitation to set me free. I accept the invitation to trade my lack of energy and my weariness for your rest. Amen."

That's it. In the beginning I promised a changed you — a you who says. . .

Life may be demanding, but I'm going to meet those demands by taking care of myself;

Life may not be easy, but I'm not going to make it any harder by overloading myself;

Life may have its burdens but I know a way to be free of my burdens by bringing them to the One who really cares.

APPENDIX
Social Readjustment Rating Scale

Dr. Thomas H. Holmes, a psychiatrist at the University of Washington School of Medicine, developed the following Social Readjustment Rating Scale (*Journal of Psychosomatic Research,* **11**:213-218, 1967, Pergamon Press, Ltd.). He warns that if several items on the list occur with intensity and close to the same time, they will create an unfavorable life situation. His list ends with minor violations of the law. I have added some further stress points discussed in this book and have left it for you to determine their degree of impact (number) on your life. Feel free to add to or subtract from the number of points assigned to each item on Dr. Holmes' scale. The scale is based on the composite scoring of many people.

Use your sum total of points as a warning beacon. If 300 points of stress — or even close to that — are occurring in your life, you need to drastically readjust your lifestyle to compensate for the loss of emotional energy you have sustained.

Stress	Points
Death of spouse	100
Divorce	73
Marital separation from mate	65
Detention in jail or other institution	63
Death of a close family member	63
Major personal injury or illness	53
Marriage	50
Being fired at work	47
Marital reconciliation with mate	45
Retirement from work	45
Major change in the health or behavior of a family member	44
Pregnancy	40
Sexual difficulties	39
Gaining a new family member (through birth, adoption, older person moving in, etc.)	39
Major business readjustment (merger, reorganization, bankruptcy, etc.)	39
Major change in financial state (a lot worse off or a lot better off than usual)	38
Death of a close friend	37
Changing to a different line of work	36
Major change in the number of arguments with spouse (either a lot more or a lot less than usual regarding child-rearing, personal habits, etc.)	35
Taking out a mortgage or loan for a major purchase (for a home, business, etc.)	31

Foreclosure on a mortgage or loan	30
Major change in responsibilities at work (promotion, demotion, lateral transfer)	29
Son or daughter leaving home (marriage, attending college, etc.)	29
Trouble with in-laws	29
Outstanding personal achievement	28
Wife beginning or ceasing work outside the home	26
Beginning or ceasing formal schooling	26
Major change in living conditions (building a new home, remodeling, deterioration of home or neighborhood)	25
Revision of personal habits (dress, manners, associations, etc.)	24
Trouble with the boss	23
Major change in working hours or conditions	20
Change in residence	20
Changing to a new school	20
Major change in usual type and/or amount of recreation	19
Major change in church activities (a lot more or a lot less than usual)	19
Major change in social activities (clubs, dancing, movies, visiting, etc.)	18
Taking out a mortgage or loan for a lesser purchase (for a car, TV, freezer, etc.)	17
Major change in sleeping habits (a lot more or a lot less sleep, or a change in part of day when asleep)	16
Major change in number of family get-togethers (a lot more or a lot less than usual)	15

Major change in eating habits (a lot more or a lot less food intake, or very different meal hours or surroundings)	15
Vacation	13
Christmas	12
Minor violations of the law (traffic tickets, jaywalking, disturbing the peace, etc.)	11

Additional Stresses

Pain in child or grandchild's life
Trouble in child or grandchild's life
Handicap or sickness of someone in your care
Unconfessed major sin
Unforgiveness, bitterness, resentment
Remarriage
Remarriage with children involved
Marriage to an alcoholic/drug-dependent person
Your own alcohol/drug dependence
Being single and living alone
Extra people in your home (including adult children)
Loving someone who does not love you
Living in a controlled situation
Working in a controlled situation
Not having time for yourself
Trouble in your church
A feeling of not being good enough
Not being appreciated
Not being understood
Not being needed

MORE BOOKS FOR WOMEN